Power of the Magdalene

The Hidden Story of the Women Disciples

Stuart Wilson and Joanna Prentis

OZARK
MOUNTAIN
PUBLISHING

For permission, or serialization, condensation, adaptions, or for our catalog of other publications, write to: Ozark Mountain Publishing, Inc., P.O. Box 754, Huntsville, AR 72740, Attn: Permissions Department.

Library of Congress Cataloging-in-Publication Data
Wilson, Stuart - 1937 -
Prentis, Joanna - 1943 -
    "Power of the Magdalene" by Stuart Wilson and Joanna Prentis
Eyewitness accounts of the relationship of Jeshua and Mary Magdalene and the other female disciples. Up-to-date information on the New Children coming to Earth now. The information was gained through regressive hypnosis, conducted by Joanna Prentis. Includes Bibliography and Index.
1. Mary Magdalene 2. Jeshua 3. Hypnosis 4. Reincarnation 5. Female Disciples 6. New Children
I. Wilson, Stuart, 1937 - II. Prentis, Joanna, 1943 - III. Mary Magdalene
IV. Title
Library of Congress Catalog Card Number: 2008940343
ISBN: 978-1-886940-59-8

Cover Design: enki3d.com
Book Design: Julia Degan
Book Set in: Times New Roman

Published By

OZARK
MOUNTAIN
PUBLISHING

PO Box 754, Huntsville, AR 72740
800-935-0045 or 479-738-2348 fax: 479-738-2448

WWW.OZARKMT.COM
Printed in the United States of America

Table of Contents

Part Six: Past Life in Translation

Part Seven: The New Children

Part Eight: A New Dawn

Part Nine: Conclusion

Part One:

The Essene Family

Joanna: So have all the Essenes made a vow to return to Earth together at the end of the cycle?
Daniel: Some have gone on to work upon higher levels, but many will return. Old friends will recognize each other, and many a tear of joy will be shed as we meet again.

The Essenes, Children of the Light, Chapter 44

1

The Story Begins

Joanna writes: It all began in 1988 when, with my daughter Tatanya, I set up the Starlight Centre in the West of England, a Centre focusing on healing and the expansion of consciousness. Two years later Stuart joined us to help with the development of the Centre, and he writes about this period:

It was inspiring and fascinating but also exhausting! A stream of visitors came in to the Centre, mainly from the United States and Australia, but some also from Europe. We had an amazing and mind-expanding time sitting at the feet of internationally respected spiritual teachers and workshop leaders.

What I remember most about this time was the big gatherings when our friends came in to share a meal and talk about our experiences and all the changes that were happening in our lives. It was a wonderful time, full of joy and laughter, and the special events – like Anna Mitchell Hedges sharing her crystal skull, a Magnified Healing workshop with Gisele King, and the two fire-walks led by Essassani – were simply magical!

When I went on to train as a past life therapist with Ursula Markham, this gave the Centre a new focus, and a whole cycle of past life regression began. Although we explored a number of historical periods, our work took a new direction through the gradual accumulation of seven past life subjects who had lives two thousand years ago in Israel. Most of these people were Essenes, and they told a remarkable story that ran parallel with the traditional account, but also contained some striking differences. The Essenes were one of the main groups within Judaism at that time. They were idealistic and dedicated people who grouped together in communities well away from the towns and villages.

Watching the Essene story unfold was an incredible experience for both of us. Within the seven subjects there were two pairs of friends, and we were able to put each pair into regression together so that they could dialogue freely. This proved to be a vital part of the process as it formed a key enabling us to penetrate the Essene veil of secrecy. The Essenes were reluctant to talk openly to other people, but they were quite happy to talk to each other! We watched as the accounts wove together, reinforcing and confirming each other as they painted a picture of Essene life.

The information which emerged from this process included the location of the main Essene communities, and the existence of a secret Core Group. There were also fascinating links with the Druids, and the first tentative glimpses of the work of the female disciples, vital pioneers of early Christianity who had been written out of the historical record.

The Essenes turned out to be very different from the traditional perception. Yes, there were the strict Essene priests who are represented in the Dead Sea Scrolls, but there were also lay brothers who studied teachings from Egypt, Persia and Greece, and parents with children who were focusing mainly on the priorities of family life. But it was the practical, emotional and humorous side of the Essene story that impressed us most. Here were real people with feelings and emotions, and it's this aspect more than any other which lifts them out of history and brings them to life for us.

With all this information being revealed it had become such an interesting story that we felt we would like to communicate it to a wider audience, and this led to our book *The Essenes,*

Children of the Light being published in March 2005.

Working with past lives continued, including one session in German, thanks to a brilliant translator. And soon we were accumulating more new information on Mary Magdalene and the female disciples.

The really big breakthrough which transformed the whole process was the dialogue which developed with an angelic being called Alariel. We discovered Alariel through a past life recall, and we describe how this happened in Chapter 3. The dialogue with Alariel added a new dimension to the process, and opened windows on many areas that we just wouldn't have been able to access otherwise.

The wide-ranging nature of the information that emerged from this dialogue, together with its consistency and clarity, revealed many new possibilities. Alariel's evidence enabled us to extend our research and fill in many gaps in the past life record. With the commentaries by Alariel running parallel with the main body of our past life work, we were beginning to cover the ground more thoroughly and in greater depth. And eventually when we had accumulated a total of seven past life subjects, we found we had enough material for this second book.

Producing this book proved to be a challenging – and at times exhilarating – journey. Now we invite you to share in this journey, following the clues from the past and exploring the many possibilities that are opening up for the future.

2

Linking with the Essene Family

Throughout our first book we used the conventional name Jesus to indicate Jeshua benJoseph. As our researches in this area continued it seemed inappropriate to use such a late and Romanized form of his name, especially as he would never have been called 'Jesus' within his own lifetime. So throughout this present book we have kept to the original Aramaic name of Jeshua, except in direct quotations from written sources. Jeshua, together with the Hebrew form Yeshua, and the name benJoseph – literally, "the son of Joseph" – were the names most often used by his contemporaries: they carry an authenticity that no later form can equal.

When *The Essenes, Children of the Light* was published, a number of people commented on the energy which the book contained, an energy which seemed to reach out and link with members of the Essene family who are now in incarnation. The book passed from one friend to another in a very timely and guided way, and soon we were getting emails from new friends living all over the world. Again, we were to meet up with many wonderful and interesting people.

One important link was with Cathie Welchman, a therapist who lives only a few miles from us. Cathie trained as a past life therapist with Dolores Cannon, and she takes copies of our book with her when she goes to Mind-Body-Spirit events with her Angel and Gem Essences. From the contacts which Cathie made at these events, other links began to form. One such link was made in the Brighton area with Bina, and when she traveled to Devon for a past life session with Cathie, another interesting piece of the jigsaw fell into place.

Bina experienced an Essene life as 'little Joseph,' who was aged 27 at the time of the crucifixion. He knew Daniel (the central character in our first book) and said that during the period immediately following the crucifixion, both of them tried to write a simple account of the life and teaching of Jeshua. However, in both cases the scrolls were found and destroyed by the Pharisees. Apparently the High Priest of the temple in Jerusalem had ordered the destruction of any documents referring to Jeshua; he clearly wished to remove all trace of him from the historical record.

This answered one of the questions which had been forming in our minds. We knew that according to current scholarship Mark's Gospel had been written in about 60-70 CE, and the other Gospels between that time and 110 CE. (See the Glossary under AD/BC.) But why did it all take so long? Why weren't some simple accounts of the life and teaching of Jeshua starting to circulate during the two decades following the crucifixion? Now it has become clear that a number of these accounts were being written, but they were destroyed whenever the Pharisees were able to find them.

This discovery has also shed some light on our present lives. It partly explains Stuart's determination to write about this period, if as Daniel, his attempts to do so had been frustrated.

Another important link was made with Gaynel Andrusko in Colorado. Her email in April 2005 was the first we received from a reader of the book. Gaynel writes:

Dear Joanna and Stuart,

Thank you for your book, *The Essenes, Children of the Light*! Your book has important information for mankind, and is so helpful for our personal happiness and growth. The subsequent church that evolved since Jesus is so different from Jesus' intentions. Please never be cautious to print this information. I and many others have some "knowing inside" and we really appreciate your getting this information to us.

Much gratitude,
Gaynel Andrusko.

Gaynel also gave us a series of most interesting questions, and we will come back to these in Chapter 14.

Jim in Brisbane, Australia was another major contact for us. Jim emailed us to say that he had been a minister of religion for nine years and that, "Jesus has guided and taught me according to what I could handle. I left the church years ago and my doctrines underwent massive changes ...

"With regard to the healing. Up until recent years I had simply been laying hands on people and releasing the healing energy. Then Jesus showed me another simple way. I would take another's hands in mine and as I began to release energy I could use my imagination to take them to a higher vibration. I would imagine their body in the next highest dimension where everything is instantaneous. Once I felt that their body was comfortable and resident in this state, I would again imagine their body restored to wholeness in the ensuing moments and release energy for this. When I felt that this had been achieved, I would imagine them and feel them back into the physical as whole. Imagination works together with the emotion in order to create this truth.

"Jesus was busy de-programming me from the past and bringing new challenges and understanding ...

"I had not believed in reincarnation, but after a series of events and articles, I could no longer deny it. I find it curious that while the orthodox believers of the Christian, Judaic and Islamic

9

faiths do not believe in reincarnation, it is an accepted doctrine of the spiritual levels of those faiths. The Christian mystic, the Jewish kabbalist and the Islamic Sufi all embrace this doctrine.

"Over the years, I gradually felt that I had a close relationship to Jesus spanning time. I just knew I was back there with him, somehow. Recently, when I was out in semi-arid country doing a bit of mining for opal, I was having lucid dreams nightly in the early hours of the morning. Then one night I went into what I knew as a past life. I was an Essene in the Qumran community, about which I knew things, even after I awoke. I was dressed in what appeared as a brown-purple robe and I relished the study." Jim goes on to say that his daughter has also been having experiences of a life in Qumran, and he intends to write this story and bring it out into the world.

Jim says this has all been a profoundly transformative experience for him, and has opened up a whole new world to explore. He writes:

"As the Light increases and awareness grows, we experience joyful triumph of this work. We can no longer afford to feed any sacred cows in the northern paddock. Our minds must open to that which IS, for this is not *belief* in something. It is that which simply IS. We must each take responsibility for our personal journey. The Universe will always bring to you the answers you seek and today we are surrounded by the clouds of witnesses from many dimensions and places in the Universe, many of whom are also able to assist us. Your vibration in soul and body will rise in line with the unlimitedness of your thought."

We love the phrase "sacred cows in the northern paddock". In its direct and very Australian way, this sums up the whole problem of entrenched resistance to change.

About the same time we made a link with Margaret: she had been born in Australia but was living in London, and during February 2007 she came to Devon to do a past life session with

Joanna. It took a little while for Margaret to get into her life as a woman living in Israel two thousand years ago, but there was a definite shift in energy when she started talking about Jeshua.

Margaret: Whenever I think about him, tears come and there is emotion...and there are times when I feel completely overwhelmed by this huge feeling of love...There's this huge emotion and there's this part of me that feels the need to teach because it's just so simple, it's so simple ...I'm just here to teach people to love each other...And it's just such a strong feeling ...so many didn't understand...I just feel so connected...you can see so clearly...it's like being home....

All these links contributed information and support, with a growing number of interconnections between friends who had shared a deep and meaningful life focused around Jeshua. That life had been intense and dramatic, and sometimes the rediscovery of it was just as dramatic, as the closeness of the soul group made itself felt, and the link with Jeshua worked its magic in the heart.

Amidst all this activity our past life work continued, with one subject coming from as far away as Germany, thanks to our friend Isabel Zaplana who proved to be a brilliant translator. And when seven subjects had completed their regressions, we reviewed the information and discovered that we had gathered enough material for this second book.

11

Part Two:

Alariel

You are constantly being challenged
to expand your awareness
and reach out into
new frequencies of consciousness,
new perspectives of truth,
new possibilities of being.

Alariel in Chapter 28.

3

First Meeting with Alariel

We have been writing these books very much on the basis of our inner guidance and have learned to trust that guidance over the years. And there was one instance when our guidance helped us to open a door to greater knowledge that would otherwise have been closed to us. It came about like this: Stuart had been exploring a life when he had been an architect called Anquel, who lived on Atlantis some time before the Golden Age. (Atlantis was the legendary ancient continent which was reputed to cover much of what is now the Atlantic Ocean.)

This life had provided a good deal of interesting information, but we were surprised and excited when our guidance told us that Anquel also had access to a much more profound and significant source. And we were told that our best chance of accessing this source would be to ask Anquel a question which we knew he would be unable to answer.

So we started casting about for a suitable question to ask. We already knew that Anquel had an interest in a "slow meditational form of movement" and this sounded to us something like an Atlantean form of Tai Chi. Taking this as our starting point, we then constructed a question along the lines that our guidance had suggested, and put this to Anquel.

Joanna: We are interested in the slow meditational form of movement which you mentioned. There is a group of people called the Essenes who live many thousands of years in the future from your time. We understand that the Essenes have a form of meditational movement and wonder if you could research this for us.

Anquel: I have never heard of these people, and if they exist in the future, I would have no way of researching this information by conventional means. However, I do have an angelic source who might be able to help. I will ask him to speak to you directly.

There followed a long pause and I had the sense of a different energy begin to focus through Stuart. Then the communication began again.

This is Alariel, speaking for a group of twelve angels who work with the Order of Melchizedek. We understand you have a question concerning the Essenes, a Brotherhood which is known to us.

Comment by Stuart: We were aware of Melchizedek because of our work on our first book. The Order of Melchizedek is a service order of advanced Teachers working on many planetary systems. We devoted Part Fifteen of *The Essenes, Children of the Light* to a discussion of the Order.

The session continues:

Joanna: Thank you, Alariel. Yes, we would like to know if the Essenes practiced a kind of slow meditational form of movement.

Alariel: Yes, but only in the northern group of communities. There were seven sequences of movement, each having a symbolic significance. These are:
> *Earth, represented by the lion,*
> *Water, represented by the fish,*
> *Fire, represented by the dragon,*
> *Air, represented by the dove,*
> *Body, represented by the bear,*
> *Mind, represented by the wolf,*

Spirit, represented by the eagle.

The movement of all these creatures was imitated in the sequences, and the whole form gave the sense of gathering all of creation into one unified flow of energy. This form came out of the work of a group of Essenes who lived at Mount Carmel. The accommodation there was more confined than that experienced at the larger communities which covered a greater area of land, and there was a need to develop a system which would exercise the body in a small space. So it was that special need that gave rise to this form and it did spread to some other communities in the northern group, but it was not widely practiced.

Joanna: Thank you, Alariel, that is most interesting. You say that you speak for a group of angels. Is there anything else about yourself that you would like to tell us, your position in the angelic world, for example?

Alariel: We work as a group and do not focus on the personal level. In the angelic world, it is the work that is important, not the individual angel.

Joanna: Could you please tell us some more about your group, then?

Alariel: The members of our group have worked with the Melchizedek Order on a number of planetary systems over a long period of time. It is our joy and privilege to work with the Melchizedeks because they are so focused on the Light. Since we became specialized in our work, it was considered appropriate that we should dialogue with groups such as your own, who have an interest in the work of the Order.

Joanna: Are there any limits to these dialogues that you can foresee?

Alariel: These communications will be limited more by your ability to conceive and phrase questions than by our ability to answer them. We respond to what is asked, and if you don't ask specific questions you are likely to get only general answers. The more specific the questions are, the more they

17

will bring forth information on the things you are interested in. As these dialogues continue you may find the quality of the questions increases and so more interesting answers will emerge. The Universe is vast, and there are some areas of knowledge that go beyond our experience, but much remains for you to explore.

Joanna: Well, thank you for this chance to dialogue with you. We shall try to come up with some good questions. I gather from what you have already told us that you have an interest in the Essenes.

Alariel: Of course. We are interested in all Melchizedek operations, and the Essenes were particularly significant because they lived at an important time for your planet. The cycle downwards into material density had to be brought to a close and the upward spiral into Light had to begin. The Essenes played a major part in this whole process. They were the main focus of Melchizedek activity on your planet at that time.

Joanna: So the Essenes were really quite advanced in many ways?

Alariel: Yes, but that is not surprising when you consider that they had, directly and indirectly, the guidance of Melchizedek teachers. The consciousness and the technology of the Essenes were both quite advanced for their time. They even had an early form of electricity, something that your culture regards as a very recent invention, yet two thousand years ago the Essenes lit their dwellings with electric lamps.

Comment by Stuart: A diagram and description of this "Baghdad Battery" and details of a modern test on the effectiveness of this design are given in *Lost Secrets of the Sacred Ark* by Laurence Gardner.

Our next question focused on Joseph of Arimathea, one of the central characters described in our first book, *The Essenes, Children of the Light*. Joseph was one of the most powerful Jews of his generation and he controlled most of the mining of tin.

Joanna: We understand that Joseph of Arimathea played a big part in the work of the Essenes.

Alariel: Yes. He was in many ways the lynch-pin that kept the whole operation together. Joseph, and the organization he led, provided a vital transport, communication and support system without which the Essenes would not have been so effective. And his cool head and resolute leadership at times of crisis kept the Essenes together and focused them on the task in hand.

Joanna: An Essene called Daniel benEzra who is described in our book was a close friend of Joseph. Daniel told us that Joseph's father was called Joseph, too, but traditional accounts give his name as Joachim. Could you comment on this please?

Alariel: When Jews of this period assumed positions of responsibility within their social group they took a patronymic name, one example being Joseph. So a man could rise in that society to become "a Joseph" in the same way that a woman could take a matronymic name and become "a Mary". It is possible that Daniel had this custom in mind when referring to Joseph's father.

Comment by Stuart: There is confirmation of this practice in Chapter 5 of *Bloodline of the Holy Grail* by Laurence Gardner. Cathie Welchman gave us some interesting questions about Daniel and Joseph, and Joanna asked these on her behalf during a later session with Alariel.

Joanna: What did Daniel benEzra look like?

Alariel: Fairly tall, quite thin and wiry, suntanned and with a beard.

Joanna: Did he look like Joseph of Arimathea?

Alariel: Joseph was more thickset, more stocky, a heavier-boned and more substantial frame which served him well during all the long journeys he took, with all the stresses and strains

involved in traveling.
Joanna: Were Daniel and Joseph the same age?
Alariel: Joseph was one year older than Daniel.

We realized from the beginning that this contact with Alariel could be a unique opportunity for us. Here, in Alariel, we had found an angelic being who did not seem to be limited by time or space. Better still, he worked within a group of twelve angels and that might extend his knowledge. This was clearly a most useful resource and it might enable us to probe areas that had so far proved elusive. Where there were gaps in the past life record we could use Alariel's knowledge to fill these in and obtain a more complete picture.

4

An Angelic Perspective

Realizing that we had the opportunity to access a wide range of information through our contact with Alariel, we set about developing a series of questions which we hoped would prove interesting. As our attention had focused on the Essenes in our first book, we began the next session with a question about the Essene Brotherhood.

Joanna: The Essenes who are in incarnation now, what is their main task?

Alariel: Partly they are here to support a reassessment of how things were two thousand years ago, particularly in the group around Jeshua. They are here to encourage all people of goodwill within the Judaeo-Christian tradition to take a look at the whole narrative of Jeshua's life in a much broader way. In doing so, they may be able to build a bridgehead between the people actively working in Christian churches and the more progressive and liberated people for whom new ideas and new perspectives seem quite natural.

Joanna: Many Christians may find "new ideas and new perspectives" very challenging.

Alariel: Yes, but change has always been present in the Christian experience, and there are aspects of Christianity that bring the promise of renewal and a fresh beginning. In particular, there are a number of groups that are now focusing on the testimony of the female disciples and the central importance of Mary Magdalene. Mary's story has enormous potential to move people out of their old rigid ideas and into a new understanding of the role played by women at that time. This not only provides a refreshing new perspective, but it also starts to build an "alternative history" to put alongside the traditional accounts. In time, this may even lead to a reassessment of Jeshua and his teachings.

Joanna: What do you see as the outcome of the teachings of Jeshua? Where was all this leading to and what was he trying to do?

Alariel: What he was trying to do was to establish a new spiritual path, a new way of living and relating to people and to God. Using the Cosmic Energy of Love which he was anchoring into Earth reality, he was encouraging people to focus that energy through the heart center. This energy is profoundly transformative. It moves through the dry forest of the heart like a cleansing fire, sweeping away the dead wood of past experiences and all the anger, fear and hurt that people cling to. When all that has gone, it empowers the individual in expanding awareness and rising into higher frequencies of consciousness. All this re-establishes the Children of the Light in a new relationship with God.

Comment by Stuart: Light in the spiritual sense (with a capital 'L') is the Eternal Divine Light, also called the Ain Soph. This is quite distinct from the common light of star systems (with a small 'l').

The session continues:

Joanna: How do you perceive God?

Alariel: It is easier to begin by saying how we do NOT perceive God! We do not see God as being in any way gender-limited, space-limited or time-limited. Any being who was limited in any of these ways could not be the true and ultimate God. Angels perceive God as a vast Web of Consciousness and

22

Energy that permeates the Universe and IS the Universe. But that is only God manifest. God also exists beyond manifestation, when there is no physical Universe, and this level is beyond our understanding. We might borrow a term from your Native American teachers and say that this is "Great Mystery". We love and revere Great Mystery, yet don't expect ever to understand this level of God. The levels of God that are accessible to our understanding focus on Oneness, Joy and Love and so we take these as indicators of the true nature of Father-Mother God.

Comment by Stuart: In Native American tradition, Great Mystery is the ultimate Source of Creation. Great Mystery creates the Great Spirit, which in turn manifests and nourishes the whole of Creation.

The session continues:

Joanna: It has been difficult for many people to reconcile the idea of a powerful God with the existence of so much suffering in the world. Why would God allow so much suffering to exist?

Alariel: God, working through the agency of the angelic host, constructs the Universe you see around you, but has given human beings free will upon the Earth. So God is like an architect designing a theater in which you sit. Now, if you do not enjoy the play you are watching, is it logical to blame the architect of the theater? Of course not. You have free will, which is essentially the right to be wrong. You have exercised this right for a long while, and have inflicted suffering upon others and upon yourselves, but if you were offered the choice of ceasing to exercise free will, we do not think you would choose that.

So it comes down to this:
God built the theater,
but you're responsible for the play.

23

Joanna: Another way of putting it would be to say that freedom of action and an all-powerful God are incompatible.

Alariel: God is indeed all-powerful in the creation of the Universe, but you can choose how you experience this Universe. You have free will to explore all the possibilities of life in your own way, but some choices may involve suffering.

Of course it would be possible to create a world where no one suffered because everyone was like a puppet with God (or the angelic agents of God) pulling all the strings. Would you be happy living in such a world? And would it have created the rich tapestry of spiritual development and creative genius that humanity has demonstrated? We think not. It would be a very safe and boring world with few possibilities for spiritual growth and it was always God's intention that you should develop to fulfill your greatest spiritual potential, evolving over long periods of time to take your place eventually amongst the Elohim.

Joanna: Please tell us something about the Elohim.

Alariel: The Elohim appear in many traditions, sometimes under the name of Great Angels or Great Spirit-Beings. They can be regarded as the Architects of the Universe, planning and supervising creation and working to bring it back into the Greater Harmony.

As the Universe is linked together in one vast Web of Consciousness and Being, the whole system must move as one. Your galaxy is now beginning to return to Source by ascending into the Light, and to keep pace with this a good deal of help is being given to planet Earth at this time under the direction of the Elohim.

Joanna: What do you see as the greatest contrast between the human and angelic worlds?

Alariel: Our world is ordered, but predictable. The human world may seem chaotic, but it is vibrant, full of conscious creative will, and the results of that creativity constantly surprise us.

24

You are always producing new solutions to problems, and your ingenuity and ability to come up with creative solutions is something we marvel at. Only the highest ranks of the angelic world are required to show this level of creativity. For the great bulk of angels within the host, it is more important that we follow the plan already given with a caring and loving attitude, working for the good of all concerned.

Joanna: Do angels experience emotion?

Alariel: We respond to some frequencies which you might regard as emotional, such as compassion, and sadness when beings turn towards darkness, and joy when they turn back to the Light. But the more basic emotions such as fear, anger, hatred and envy, we do not resonate to. If you feel constantly nourished, loved and sustained by the Source of all, and live and move within the Oneness of that Source, these basic emotions simply have no meaning.

Joanna: How do you experience time?

Alariel: Time does exist in the angelic world, but not time as you know it. Our time consists of one thing following another – a series of sequences if you like, which is why we call it sequential time. Your time also has sequential elements in it, but it is rigid, or at least rigid as far as most humans are concerned. Our sequential time is not rigid, it is very flexible indeed. We can return to any part of it, and rerun any segment of it, but within that segment, the sequences will follow one another in a logical order, they will not be scrambled in a random fashion. We would not be able to implement the plans given by the Elohim if time was random and haphazard, so that no sequence followed any other sequence in a logical order. It is just that the ordering of the sequences is one thing and the accessing of them is another. We respect the ordering, but can access any sequence at will.

We see consciousness as One, and evolving towards the One again, but in between these points of Oneness going through apparent separation, "manyness" and linear time as you know it. The rigid linear part of time we see as the middle stage of spiritual evolution, the one that you are passing through now. When you move on to your next stage of development, you will see time as much more flexible and events within any sequence as much more accessible than you do at present. Certain human beings with special skills, like a trained shaman for example, may be able to perceive time in this more flexible way, but these skills are comparatively rare amongst humans at this stage of your development.

Joanna: Do angels pray?

Alariel: It depends upon what you mean by prayer. Praying in the sense of asking Father-Mother God for something – very rarely. Praying in the sense of attunement to God, God's will, design, purpose – yes, all the time. Our work would not be possible without constant attunement. Sadly, human beings do not understand attunement. They think of it as simply aligning with the Divine Will, but it's more complex than that. There is a Divine Plan, a blueprint for the whole creation, and the angelic host works to manifest that blueprint, first in creation and then in sustaining what is created and in assisting in the spiritual evolution of manifested beings. This blueprint is a combination of firm principles and flexible application of those principles, so it is not a totally fixed and rigid system.

At any time, in the light of unfolding events, an angel may attune and ask that the plan be changed and modified. In planetary systems where there are varying degrees of free will, this is essential, for free will often changes the pattern of things quite substantially.

When an angel puts forward a possible change to the existing plan, this is considered within the angelic host and either:

> *(a) immediately accepted and implemented,*
> *(b) put forward for investigation by a panel of angels expert in this area, or*
> *(c) assigned to a conference of angels with a wide range of abilities and experience. This is essential when a very major change is proposed.*

Joanna: How can we best encourage change on this planet? Do you think we should fight or oppose old organizations which are resisting change?

Alariel: Be aware that whenever you fight something, you are focusing on it and giving it energy. If you wish to remove something from manifestation, it is better to focus on its opposite: give that good quality or organization energy, and watch it flourish and grow, knowing that the old will wither away in its own time.

Joanna: The concept of "soul aspects" is still a difficult one for many people. Could you give your perception of this please?

Alariel: During the early stages of human evolution it was sufficient for the soul to put down one part of itself, one incarnated presence, upon the Earth at a time. Then as the civilizations on the Earth developed and became more complex, offering a wider range of spiritual experience, many souls wished to access several of these possibilities at the same time. The solution was for the soul to put down several personalities or aspects – often as many as twelve at one time. The memories of all twelve personalities feed back into the soul, and in subsequent lives all later aspects of that soul would remember these lives.

Joanna: What element of human consciousness that we have lost is it important for us to bring back now?

Alariel: Undoubtedly, it is the Goddess element: the Sacred Feminine is the source of the highest and most subtle wisdom, and the most profound Knowing. Shamanic cultures have always recognized the primacy of feminine wisdom, and it is time that this primacy – symbolized by Mary Magdalene – is more widely acknowledged in the world. It is only by acknowledging the primacy of feminine wisdom that conflicts will be resolved and the deep wounds that humanity has inflicted upon itself over the centuries will finally begin to heal.

Joanna: What do you think is the greatest human failing?

Alariel: To go into instant judgment about many people and many things. This is particularly marked when you are thinking about the outcome of any of your actions. In many human situations you are in a position that we would describe as IDA0 – Insufficient Data to Assess the Outcome. Yet you continually try to judge what the result of your actions might be, and worse still, punish yourselves when the outcome is not as you have predicted. There are so many variables on a planet where free will dominates that frankly it is foolish to predict a single outcome in any situation. Predict a whole range of possible outcomes if you must, but even then something may happen that you had not foreseen and therefore could not predict. As timelines moving into the future are so subtle and so subject to change, it would be a much wiser course for you to predict nothing, but simply observe what happens as time moves on.

Joanna: And what do you think is the greatest strength of human beings?

Alariel: Their ability to respond with love in their hearts to others – human beings, animals or plants – when these are in difficulty or pain. It is the unique human heart quality that will carry you through, for it has the ability to sweep away all the dross of selfishness and greed. When human beings feel and act with their hearts, they are capable of making remarkable breakthroughs.

Part Three:

The Essene Drama Unfolds

Angel of Harmony,
help us to tune our lives this day
to Mother Earth and Father Sun:
help us to work with joy
and share all that we have with love,
so that when evening comes,
we may find peace.

> Stuart Wilson
> A Morning Attunement inspired by
> the Essene Communions.

5

James in Israel and Egypt

About the same time as our first book was published, Joanna booked herself in for a past life session with our friend Cathie Welchman, and a few weeks later, Cathie came to see us for a reciprocal session. Joanna put her into an altered state and asked her to connect with any life she may have had in the Middle East about two thousand years ago. Once she had connected with a life at that time, Joanna asked her what she could see.

Cathie: The ground is dry and dusty...I'm seeing palm-trees ...now I can see houses...It's hot...I think I'm going to a meeting...I'm expecting to see someone there...I see a seat, a bench built into the wall, and there's a man there, motioning for me to be quiet...I sit down beside him.

    Just round the corner to my left I can see a courtyard, and a lot of Light in it. It seems to be an inner group, and they're in the Light...in a circle on the ground, dressed in long robes, and they're...in some sort of communion ...linking in some way. And there is one who stands out – it's as if he glows – and I'm watching him. I'm not very old, about thirteen, sitting in the shadows...just watching these other people there. I can't hear what the speaker is saying ...the Light is all around his head, like a rose color, and they're receiving color from him. How I'd like to be a part of this...I know I should be there, I have been guided to be there.

Comment by Stuart: By the time the whole story had unfolded, it became clear that "the speaker" was in fact Jeshua benJoseph. At this point, probably some time during his Ministry, Jeshua was probably connecting with a number of groups such as this one. The Light round his head must have been his aura.

The session continues:

Cathie: Now the speaker has left the group and approached me. He's telling me my time will come. I'm only thirteen and I know I will have to go to Mary first.
Joanna: Which Mary is this?
Cathie: Mary Salome.

Comment by Stuart: Mary Salome was one form of the name of Helena Salome, a sister of Mother Mary (see Chapter 9.)

The session continues:

Joanna: What is your name?
Cathie: I am called James.

(Now that James has identified himself we will use that name.)

Joanna: What is this place called?
James: It's called Gedi, Ein Gedi. I live near it.

Comment by Stuart: Ein Gedi was one of the southern group of Essene communities which was identified in Chapter 6 of *The Essenes, Children of the Light*. (See Diagram.)

The session continues:

Joanna: What happens at Ein Gedi?

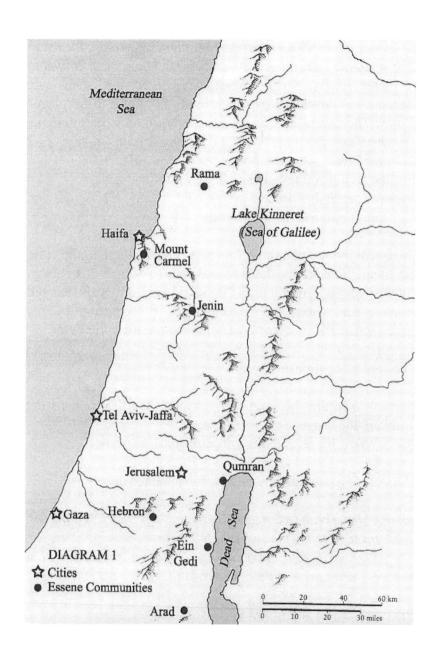

Mediterranean
Sea

Rama ●

Lake Kinneret
(Sea of Galilee)

Haifa ☆
Mount ●
Carmel

Jenin ●

☆Tel Aviv-Jaffa

Jerusalem☆   Qumran
                ●
☆Gaza Hebron
          ●

DIAGRAM 1   Ein ●
☆ Cities   Gedi
● Essene Communities

Dead Sea

Arad ●

| 0 | 20 | 40 | 60 km |
| 0 | 10 | 20 | 30 miles |

33

*James: I dont know much about what happens there. I visit
sometimes ...I know Jeshua goes there sometimes. I listen to
my guide so I can go when he visits...I have been guided to
go there since I was very young.*

Joanna: How do your parents feel about you coming to this place?

*James: They know it's something special...if they can't find me,
they know I've gone there. My parents are kind, they give me
much freedom and allow me to use my gifts.*

Joanna: Could you tell me about your gifts?

*James: I see lights around people and I know who is safe and
who is not, who is dangerous.*

Comment by Stuart: I think James is referring here to the aura,
the energy field around the head and body of every human being.
Anyone who can see auras and is skilled in reading them can tell
a good deal about the consciousness of a person by the
arrangement and movement of colors within the auric field.

The session continues:

Joanna: Who are the dangerous people? Are the Romans the
problem, the danger?

James: No ...it's the leaders of our people, the priests...

(There was a pause here while Cathie breathed deeply.)

*James: I have been to Ein Gedi again, but this time it is different.
I must go to my parents and tell them we must go to Egypt,
where we'll find Mary Salome. I know there's something
very wrong now. I don't understand, but it's not right for us
to be here any more.*

Joanna: Are you still thirteen?

*James: I'm still thirteen, but we must leave...the energy has
changed, completely changed. It felt good before, but
everything's different now...there's a big shift in energy as if*

34

something is breaking and moving apart, moving on...I have to go back to my parents. They sense the energy has changed and ask me what's the matter. And I tell them I've seen Jeshua, but not as I would expect to see him. The energy is different...Something has happened to him, I don't know what it is...When he came to the group, his feet had big holes in them and it scared me.

Joanna: Nobody told you what happened to him?

James: No. But I know something has changed about him. Jeshua said we all have to go and go quickly. The followers of Jeshua are in danger...the priests will root out anyone connected with Jeshua. The followers will be in great danger and we must leave. My parents say, can we delay a little and tell our friends, but I say we must get the pack animal, the mule, and leave right away. Make our way to Egypt and we will be guided.

Comment by Stuart: James sounded quite anxious and confused at this point. It is not clear whether he was seeing Jeshua himself, or an image of Jeshua when he was bilocating. (Later in this book we had confirmation that Jeshua was able to bilocate and appear in two places at the same time.) If this event which James is describing happened after the crucifixion, then he was probably seeing a bilocated image.

The session continues:

(Here there was a long pause, and a sense of time passing in the life of James.)

We've traveled a long way now.. .we've met people who are dressed like us, but I know they're not just ordinary travelers because they have Light around them. We've met people of the Light all along the way... We are taken in along the way by other people who see our Light...but we must find Mary

Salome and she'll tell us where to go next.

Joanna: Do you know much about Mary Salome?

James: She's one of the inner circle around Jeshua.

Joanna: What is your mother's name?

James: My mother's real name is Elizabeth, but we call her Liza.

Joanna: What about Joseph of Arimathea? Is he known to your family?

James: Yes, he's a friend of my family. He's very old and he's given me some instructions on sailing.

Joanna: Is he one of the teachers of the Essenes?

James: Only for those who are interested in foreign lands and traveling, the Celtic lands far away across the sea...he has a different Light around him...mainly concentrated around the head and neck...in rainbow circles, blue and pink and violet and it's very pretty...

Comment by Stuart: An interesting section because it shows how different things look to a thirteen-year-old. No doubt Joseph taught many things, but for a boy the interesting things would be ships and travel to exotic foreign lands, so that's what Joseph talked about when he saw James.

The session continues:

Joanna: Have you reached Egypt now?

James: Yes. ... the energy is quite different in Egypt. So much has been gathered and learned here and my parents like it here. We've reached Alexandria, we call it "Alysene" and there are piles of food and fat goats and the people live well here.

Joanna: So in the area you came from, the food was scarce?

James: It was. We didn't have a lot of food but what we had was shared equally.

Joanna: So this is a better place?

James: Yes, very prosperous. The people look happy, they have rounded faces, and they're not scared.

Comment by Stuart: As we discovered during the research for *The Essenes, Children of the Light*, Alexandria (at Lake Mareotis) was one of the original or "main stem" Essene communities. As such, it was a natural place for Essenes in trouble to head towards. There were few safe havens in the Essene world, but the community at Alexandria was certainly one of them.

The session continues:

Joanna: How long do you stay in Alysene?

James: We must wait while my parents recover from the journey. And we need to find out what is happening with the group around Jeshua.

Joanna: When you were younger, were you able to spend some time with Jeshua?

James: Yes. He knew my parents and would sometimes come to the house and talk...tell parables, and would talk and talk and then play with the children afterwards. You could see his energy affecting all the people.

Joanna: As a small child, did you feel you got more from the energy than the words?

James: Of course. I didn't understand some of his words. I was too young, but I watched the Light. As the people there understood what he was saying, it increased the Light all around them. When they absorbed information from Jeshua, it was like a great explosion of Light in all directions. And he would also send geometric patterns to people who didn't have the Light. I watched the Light and saw the angels around him. There was a special kind of laughter at these meetings, a laughter in the heart.

I liked to be with him, and I was so proud to be there. Jeshua would come on his journeys for a rest, but he would never get that rest because people wanted to talk to him. Word would get around that he was there and the people would come to see him and listen. He had a very soft voice and you had to be quiet to hear him. It made you calm to hear him. He would have this soft voice when meeting with people and healing their hearts.

His hair was sort of wild. Other people made their hair beautiful...combed and held in place...but Jeshua never did anything to his hair...it was almost a mane. It was clean, but it was unbrushed, a kind of brown with copper lights in it, and his eyes were blue and very intense.

Joanna: So you're still in Alexandria, Alysene?

James: Yes. We've found out that Mary Salome has been here, but has already left. The people we're staying with tell us that Herod was forced to do something to Jeshua ...(sobs)...it's too horrible...I don 't know exactly what happened, but the priests were behind it.

Joanna: Yes, Jeshua had some sharp words with them...

James: He told them to change their ways, he told them to change, but they wouldn't. Jeshua told us that different times were coming. . . the priests were afraid they would lose their position and their importance if things changed. Jeshua said the law was symbolic, pointing the way to understanding, but they couldn't grasp that.

Joanna: The priests had fixed beliefs. They were into the head and it was hard for them to feel in the heart.

James: That's why the women understood. They intuitively understood that Jeshua was a leader and teacher of change. They understood the energy behind his teaching if not all his words.

The Essenes we're staying with know more than we do about what has been happening. We're made to feel very welcome, but my father is concerned that he has little to give them in exchange for all their hospitality and he doesn't want us to outstay our welcome.

Joanna: Does your father practice some craft?

James: Yes, he's a scribe...very skilled in languages. I understand his connection with Egypt now. He has

translated many scrolls in his life, and some of these came from Egypt.
Joanna: An Essene called Daniel benEzra also worked with scrolls. Does your father know him?
James: Yes, he is related to us.

Daniel benEzra was the main character described in our book *The Essenes, Children of the Light.* Although a number of other individuals contributed to this account of Essene life, the core of the book is Daniel's story. James thought of Daniel as an elder brother, but we were able to ask Alariel about this in a later session, and this was his response:

Alariel: They were cousins. James' grandfather was called Benjamin and he had a great interest in astrology. Benjamin had two sons who were astrological opposites, the sun sign of one brother being the rising sign of the other. He gave them names to reflect that, calling one son Ezra Nathaniel and the other son Nathaniel Ezra. When Ezra Nathaniel married he had one child, who was Daniel. Nathaniel Ezra married Sarah, but she died. He then married Elizabeth and they had one child, who was James. This is why James was so much younger than Daniel because he was the child of a second marriage.

Comment by Stuart: From this it is clear that James was a first cousin to Daniel, and not a brother.

The session continues:

James: I don't know where he is now...we haven't heard from him. Daniel is much older than I am, but he often came to see us. I told him about the Light I see around people.
Joanna: Have you a favorite story about Daniel?
James: The children liked Daniel and used to pull at his robes.

Because he'd often been traveling about with Jeshua and between the communities, he would bring little things back for the children. So they would tug at his robe and say, "You must have something!" Because Jeshua put Light into stones, Daniel got into the habit of bringing little pebbles back and he used to spread out these pebbles and say to the children, "Which one has Jeshua put the Light into?" And those children who had the gift always used to pick these ones out.

Some children would just pick a pebble because it was pretty, and they would feel hurt that they hadn't chosen the right one. But Daniel used to tell them, "The next time Jeshua comes, give him your pebble and he'll put some Light into it too," so in the end they didn't mind too much. Daniel was good with children, but he didn't really know much about children and we thought he was very serious. (Gives a sigh.) *We never saw Daniel again after we left for Egypt. I know my parents missed him, but they never spoke to him again.*

Comment by Stuart: This all helps us to get a more rounded view of Daniel, and to fill out the picture which emerged from *The Essenes, Children of the Light*. Seeing him relate to children in this way shows another facet of his character, and helps in bringing him to life for us.

It is interesting to speculate that there may still be pebbles on the beaches of Britain which Jeshua had infused with Light when he visited our shores.

6

James in Gaul and Britain

The account that James had given of his travels after the time of the crucifixion had been fascinating so far, and we were eager to hear the rest of his story. Did he go as far north as Britain? Did he encounter any Druids, and did he meet up again with Joseph of Arimathea?

James: We stayed in Alysene for some time, but at last we had to move on. I knew most of our friends would have left our land by then. The group I saw at Ein Gedi were close to Jeshua and they would certainly have gone. That group had much Light around them, particularly the women.

> *When we left, we went by ship across the central sea. We got safely across, although the passage was rough. In the land to the north, the place called Gaul, we met many others that we recognized, including Mary Salome. We landed in a small port, a pretty place that was so green. Now we're traveling up into the Celtic lands that stretch far to the north. It's cold and there is a cold wind blowing.*

James traveled north through Gaul (the present-day France) with a mixed group, most from Israel but some from Egypt and other countries in the Middle East. James commented that, "Many different people have been thrown together through fear and need, and having a path to follow." They traveled north following an important energy line (we would call it a *leyline*) which they "followed as a trail." They rode on "small horses," which we later identified as Caspians, a small, hardy breed standing about 10 to 12 hands high. James described some of the terrain as "hard and rocky" and he saw mountains, something he had never seen in Israel, and experienced snow for the first time. His group developed skills in sensing and feeling the ley-lines as they went along.

For the younger ones, "it was like a strange new adventure," but for the older ones, there was much sadness. At one point, James talked about a gathering of people who were traveling through Gaul, with a number of tents pitched on a high and open place. It was cold and they huddled around a number of fires on the site. It was a chance for them to share their memories, talk about old friends and support each other.

James: We knew we have to keep the memories alive...and that's what we're doing.

Joanna: So the teachings that you had from Jeshua, they were mainly energetic, but there were also teachings with words?

James: It wasn't for me so much teaching as showing you a way to Be. How to live as a spirit within a body, how to act and react with the people around you. A very simple message, to live in the heart and not harm others.

Oh – (there was a pause, a shift in the energy and a sudden intake of breath) *the lady called Mary is coming to our group.*

Joanna: Is this Mary Salome?

James: No it's not – it's Mary Magdalene (a deep intake of breath and a sigh.) *She's so beautiful, she has dark eyes ...she is our link with the Kaloo, and she brings messages from them. It's she who's informing our scattered people of the jobs we must do. She is telling us that it's through the female line that the emotional aspects of the memories will be held. The men are the doers and they must find information through external records, and both are needed. The men will be helped by physical records...linked through crystals and places, portals where they'll be able to access the universal records of events – real history.*

Comment by Stuart: The Kaloo were the scattered remnants of an ancient Atlantean people who founded the Essene communities under the direction of the Order of Melchizedek. We discovered a good deal of information on the Kaloo whilst researching *The Essenes, Children of the Light*, and they also appear in *Jesus and the Essenes* by Dolores Cannon. The Order of Melchizedek is a service Order of advanced Teachers working on many planetary systems throughout the galaxy.

The session continues:

Joanna: Is this the first time you've met Mary Magdalene?
James: Yes.
Joanna: And from your body reaction, the meeting obviously made a very big impression on you. Was it her energy field that particularly impressed you?
James: Yes, it's huge...it's purple and...blue. (Here Cathie was so overcome that she could hardly get the last word out.) *She links with many other beings, on the Earth and off the Earth; it's all tied in with Light, so you feel as if she's bringing a vortex of the whole universe's memory into your place.*
Joanna: Is she able to create vortexes if she settles in a place for a while?
James: I don't think she needs to, she IS the vortex.
Joanna: The other Essenes around you, are they aware that she is the one who carries the greatest energetic nearest to that of Jeshua?
James: It's different because when she's there, you are not aware of what the others are experiencing at the time. It's as if you are not in a place on Earth at all...the fire in front of us disappears, and she is bringing the whole universe in blues

and purples and yellows and that's all you're aware of, that and this majestic energy. (Again difficult for Cathie to talk at this point.)

Joanna: I know when I link up with someone with a major aura you're not aware of what they say. It's the energy, and you go into a state where anything is possible.

James: She will be a major force in making people remember what they learned then. Jeshua's job was to open the heart center. Once that's open, Mary Magdalene's job is to provide the information that's needed at the right time. She does this by showing how everyone is linked and how information can be gained when you ask for it. She doesn't talk to us in words, but everyone receives the information they need. I wish I could have had her as my teacher, then I wouldn't have needed to ask so many questions. With her, you feel as if you know the answer before you ask the question.

Joanna: So in many ways she's opening up the innate spiritual knowledge that you brought in to this life?

James: Yes.

Joanna: And for many it's just a case of re-remembering?

James: Reconnecting, yes. She travels through different dimensions in time and space ...you need special training to do this...such a special being ....

Mary is due to go on with her journey...she will be with us from time to time...she's working with John. When she's finished, it's night and the stars are out, and we hadn't realized so much time has passed. There's much excitement throughout the group as they discover they are serving a purpose, being of use.

Joanna: So night has fallen and you're looking at the stars....

James: I find it hard to sleep on this special night – there were so many things that I wanted to ask Mary Magdalene. I wanted to ask her what the deep maroon color in her aura signifies. And I wanted to get around the other groups and see what

44

they were doing. It's as if we were all laying down the pattern of what was to come for the future...real big special foundations. But I must get some sleep because at dawn we must all split up and go our separate ways.

In a later session, we asked Alariel to comment on this meeting with Mary Magdalene, and this is what he said:

Alariel: This is a good example of the kind of impact made by Mary Magdalene. Mary was an impressive speaker, but it was the energy she carried – the quality and sheer power and vastness of that energy – which really impressed those who met her for the first time. Here was a Master-soul, an Initiate who had reached the very highest levels of attainment within the Isis system of Egypt, a system that was widely respected throughout the Middle East as the mainstream Mystery School tradition at that time. So to be in the presence of a high Isis Initiate was something that many people would have seen as a great blessing.

Comment by Stuart: Isis, the high-priestess moon goddess, was one of the most important deities in the Egyptian pantheon. As the wife of Osiris and mother of Horus, she had a central position in that system, and was regarded as the goddess of magic, alchemy and supreme wisdom. She was often called upon by those who needed help with past life memories.

James and his group continued to travel northwards through Gaul. At one point, he met an impressive man whom he describes as "a sage" and this man gave him a golden Ankh, an Egyptian cross with a rounded upper section. James told us that this particular Ankh had been adapted by carving a figure of Jeshua into it.

The Ankh was a key symbol in Egyptian religion from the period of the heretic pharaoh Akhenaten, who established a form

45

of monotheism centuries before the time of Moses. The basic meaning of the Ankh is *life*.

The session continues:

James: I put it to my third eye and received images, many images. These images tell us what to do. We have got to get on with our work now. When Jeshua was among us, everyone was focused on him and what he would do and what we could gain from him...but he didn't tell anyone in detail what to do. I know we're supposed to be finding our purpose now.

Joanna: And what do you see as your purpose?

James: Sending out golden rhythms of Light through the energy lines that we learned about so that the Earth can experience the Light. That's what Jeshua was doing with the pebbles. He was helping the Earth Consciousness experience Light so that it links itself more closely with what's happening with human beings...so that it's more aware of the life on the Earth. It's like filling the earth lines with energy...energizing them. And we're telling her about the new energy Jeshua brought in so that she knows we've moved on a stage. It will go all over the Earth, every part of the Earth.

Comment by Stuart: Our modern name for the Consciousness of the Earth is "Gaia," originally a Greek name which has been widely adopted both by environmentalists and by the wider new age community.

The session continues:

James: We're all getting training, we're all getting information...So I see that my task is to continue to work with the energy lines...Put in the heart energy that we know about from Mary Magdalene – that's what she gave us –

information on that kind of energy. She gave me information to pass on. It helps us in our predicament.

Joanna: What is your predicament?

James: That we feel leaderless. Each of us has to find our purpose so that we can act on it. We go quietly through the countryside...it's beautiful, but very quiet. All we can hear is the hooves of the donkeys. We have left the little horses behind us, and we're riding on donkeys now.

We've climbed up higher and there's a building with grayish-blue tiles. There's a group of about six of us and we're going to meet this man. He has a shaven head and golden skin. He feels safe, he creates a presence of everything being in its right place. He wants to show us how to carry out our purposes. He's put a plan before us, to this group with me, nearly all young. And he shows us how to use water, and to put energy into the water with our minds or with crystals. The water sparkles almost as if it has diamonds in it...it sparkles. He shows us channels that have already been made, and says this is what the ancient Kaloo used to do. They used to put channels through a town and round a town. A kind of grid to link in with the Earth's natural energy lines and it's almost like irrigation, trying to draw the energy through the energy lines. Put it through the water in grids and then it goes back into the energy lines.

Joanna: I believe the Essenes were doing this in Israel.

James: That's how they managed to grow crops in the desert. This is how the people were kept in balance and healthy. This is how the food was grown, using the energy of the Earth via energy lines. They put it into the water. So our task is to find and map the energy lines.

Joanna: Do you use your hands to find the energy lines?

James: I just walk across them and get a tingle in my feet. So we're going to mark the important lines out with stones, big stones. And we're going to walk through Gaul.

Joanna: And are there special places where the lines meet?

47

James: All over the world, there are special places with water. Through the water, through the flow, the suffering of the Earth can be cleared and released. That's part of my work, to set up these healing places.

Joanna: Jeshua said to you, "Your time will come." Did it come?

James: Yes, when I was much older. I see myself then and I 've grown a long beard...I'm in a long dark woolen robe. I feel that it's quite cold. I've moved to the northern part of Gaul. We're setting up a spring. This is a very special place, so we're setting up almost a temple. There are crystals to make it easier for Jeshua to be linked with us...a stepping up of our energy and a stepping down of his.

Joanna: How would you sum up your task?

James: To keep the links with the energy lines through water, to keep the inner springs alive, linking with the Earth energy. To move all of that forward, to advance in spiritual understanding, to keep putting it back whenever it gets stamped out. To keep it going, to keep the links with Jeshua and Mary. For the people of Jeshua's generation, their job was to get the word out. It's my job to keep the heart center open through the Earth's energies...keeping the energetic memory alive. The Earth has a resonance linking to us, and we help the Earth so she can help us.

This part of James' account was fascinating as it shows his focus on working with earth energies, something that is not stressed very often in material on the Essenes, and is entirely absent from all the accounts of the work undertaken by the early Christian followers of Jeshua. It helps to put his teachings into a bigger context as part of the relationship between human beings and the Earth. Another significant aspect is the central importance of Mary Magdalene as the continuer of Jeshua's work, and the provider of a link between Jeshua and all the Essenes and followers of Jeshua who had settled in Gaul. At that time, there were a number of Jewish groups scattered throughout Gaul, and that country certainly provided a welcome new home for those who were fleeing persecution in Israel.

Some of the party who traveled with James continued northwards and reached Britain. For James himself, however, the journey finished in northern Gaul, where he settled down and married a woman from that area. This is James' description of her:

James: She is beautiful, tiny, and very understanding. Her name in their tongue means "Starlight".

We continue with James as he reaches the Interlife and is reviewing his life as a whole:

James: I lived until I was about sixty.
Joanna: Did you ever go to Britain?
James: Yes, and that's where I was buried. I traveled across northern Gaul and then we took a boat. I presented the people in Britain with a pair of our horses, a fine stallion and a mare. And this was in exchange for educating a group of our own people. They were to start the work in Britain. I came back and forth and visited Britain, I found it very cold. Joseph of Arimathea had gone to Britain before me, but by the time of my first visit he had already died.
Joanna: When you got to Britain, did you hear about what Joseph had done there?
James: He'd set up a school to exchange information and energies. He had some writings carved in stone. I can see many strange hieroglyphics that I don't recognize. The Druids didn't have a writing tradition, but we did, and we wished to get the information down in written form. Joseph had people carve in the stone important things. They are long thin stones, a pale brown colored stone, with a flat face and the inscriptions are put in there. Information on sacred rites and how to keep connected. When I visited Britain, it

was always a special occasion when we'd some energy work to do.

This gave us an opportunity to ask about the Druids, who were the teachers and leaders of the Celtic peoples. However, we got a very strange and unexpected answer.

Joanna: I understand the Druids were quite an advanced people, and they had large centers of learning.

James: They're a funny people, really advanced in some ways and yet they don't seem to wash very often, and we had come from a tradition where you'd bathe every day. They had vast amounts of water in Britain, but the Druids would have dirty fingernails. I saw the Light around them, and they meant well, they just weren't bothered with washing too much. But in other ways, they were extremely advanced. They knew about herbs and how to use them to cure illnesses, they were very advanced in that way. They could even carry out operations, deal with toothache and were adept at mending bones.

Joanna: How did they mend bones?

James: They splinted them with wood from a special tree – I think it was an ash. They would take the tree, slit it down and place the new wood with sap in it against the area of the break, and would attach crystals to each end of the pointed pieces of ash and channel energy, and put burning herbs on the wood and that would make it hot. The herbs were smelly, but this treatment seemed very effective in healing broken bones. They were also very adept at working with the Earth and calling down the rain. They weren't hunter-gatherers, they grew grains and were able to modify grains and mill them and make a cake from them. They gathered herbs from special places and they knew what herbs to use to get a kind of trance so they could connect with the goddesses of the land. And so I learned much from them and they learned from us.

Joanna: What was the most important event which you went to while you were in Britain?

James: I think the last event when I was there, not long before I died. We went to an area known as "Priscelly" and we set up some grey-blue stones, like slate, and these could hold certain energies of the Earth when joined in with special energy lines and quartz crystals. And since we were gathered there and all knew our purposes, we had to make sure we'd remember our purposes from lifetime to lifetime because we knew that each time we were born, we might forget them. So we had to link in with the Earth, so that when we moved over the energy lines, the grids, we would be triggered to remember, again and again, what we'd come for. And we used certain Kabalistic symbols and words to ensure that each lifetime each of us would connect. My connection is with the water and the sacred sites. Other people would link to the stones, others would link to stars and astronomy, and for others, there would be flashbacks of using their skills. So we all met together to make sure we'd be carrying out Jeshua's work until the time came when we would be released.

Comment by Stuart: The Kabala or Qabalah is the mystical system of teaching based on the Zohar or *Book of Splendours.* Kabalist teachings lie at the very heart of the Judaic tradition and they focus on the central symbol of the Tree of Life.

Now that James' story had been told, we could step back and look at it as a whole. It was a fascinating story, and it filled in a lot of gaps for us. The wonderful thing about this part of James' account is the way it illustrates how diverse the work of the followers of Jeshua could be. Spreading the teachings was only a tiny part of a much bigger spectrum of work, much of which concerned working with earth energies. For the Essenes, who had worked with earth energies for so long under the instructions of the Kaloo, that would not come as a surprise, but anyone brought up in the mainstream Jewish rabbinic tradition might find all this very strange indeed. It's also not at all the kind of work that the early Church Fathers would have known about or valued, and they would probably have dismissed it as being much too near pagan practices.

The name which James pronounced as "Priscelly" is almost certainly a reference to the Preseli mountains in south-western Wales. This area contributed the smaller bluestones at Stonehenge, and was well-known throughout the ancient world as a source of stones of the highest quality.

7

Akhira

In July 2006 Isabel Zaplana and Michael Schaefer from Burgess Hill in Sussex came to visit us to do a combined past-life session. Isabel and Michael have strong links with the channeling source Kryon, and their work with Gematria dietary supplements takes them all over the world.

After they were both taken back to a past life in the Middle East about the time of Jeshua, the first part of the session concentrated on Michael's experience as a teacher. While Michael's process moved quickly through a whole cycle of experience and release, Isabel took longer to feel her way into that life. But when she did connect with this energy, much new information emerged. We join her at the point where the session has just started moving forward quickly for her:

Isabel: I have the feeling that half of my body is buried in warm sand.. .and I'm very relaxed.. .I think it's more like a training or a healing...
Joanna: Is there one person healing you or a group?
Isabel: A group, yes.
Joanna: And what is your name?

There was a little difficulty in focusing on the exact sound of the name, but this is what eventually emerged.

Isabel: Akhira...a spiritual name given to me as part of the training.

Later, we found that her original name had been Rachel. Now that Akhira has identified herself, we will use that name. She pronounced it with a long "e" sound as "Akeerah".

Joanna: Do you feel you're in a community?
Akhira: Yes.
Joanna: Can you tell me anything about this community?
Akhira: They're very loving, and there's a very strong feeling of unity, of family. I feel very comfortable, very relaxed. It's part of the work we're doing together.
Joanna: Tell me about this work.
Akhira: We're improving ourselves...not only for ourselves...we have a mission, and we have to be healed and trained. We heal people and we heal places. The others are more advanced than me.
Joanna: Is the training in expansion of consciousness?
Akhira: It's like healing and training to become more advanced. We have a role as healers...I am a woman and I'm preparing for something important on a spiritual level. I receive very much attention from the others. They are interested in how I grow and progress. I'll have a specific role, I don't know exactly what yet, I'm young.

We discovered later in the session that Akhira was about seventeen years old at this time.

Akhira: They know what is going on and they are happy and treat me lovingly, they smile...

Joanna asked Akhira about Michael's role in this life, and she replied: *He is older than me. He is a teacher called Benjamin and is not married.*

Joanna: Can you describe the place where your community is?

Akhira: It's grouped around a temple, and it's very spiritual. I think it's in Egypt. I am from Israel, but I have been brought here for training.

Joanna: Would that be Alexandria?

Akhira: Yes, it's the highest place for this kind of training.

Joanna: In Egypt, you would not be so noticed as you would be in your homeland?

Akhira: Yes, there's more freedom here for this kind of work...more acceptance. In Israel, it's all hidden...Israel is dangerous, so they have sent me here. I need this training and I need to be safe, and I'm not safe in Israel. But I will have to work there, we all have to do our work in Israel.

Joanna: Did you know Benjamin from your time in Israel?

Akhira: Yes, I know him from Israel. He's known to my parents. He's older, more like my parents in age. He's a friend of the family and he knows very much. He's important inside the group.

Joanna: Did you ever meet Jeshua?

Akhira: Yes.

Joanna: How do you remember him?

Akhira: He came to visit us. He knew I was doing my training. I'm younger than he is. He has a very good contact with children. He's so loving...He jokes with us, he's very relaxed.

Joanna: Did you ever meet Mary Magdalene?

Akhira: Yes. She cared about us and she came to see us. She's older, but she's gone through a process and she's now very experienced and she's like a big sister. She's very respected and known to be very much of the Light. She's caring for us, she comes to see how we are. There is a very strong connection...she comes alone, she's not with Jeshua now. I've never seen them together.

Joanna: But you've heard they were together?

Akhira: Yes, I've heard...yes, they say she's with Jeshua, she's a very high being.

Joanna: Was there a spiritual marriage between Mary Magdalene and Jeshua?

Akhira: We knew they were together...

Joanna: They're both very high Initiates?

Akhira: Yes, and we're a bit nervous when she comes, but she's very natural, like a friend, a...confidante. We're very close because we know the same things, we've done the same training.

Joanna: So she's like a spiritual mentor to you?

Akhira: Yes, she knows what we know and this makes us very close. We are like her group of students. It feels as if we are her girls. It is a very peaceful moment...she's very relaxed and happy to see us. She's not staying here, but she's coming to visit us. She doesn't do specific training or ceremony with us. We don't speak very much, it's very telepathic.

Joanna: So it's an exchange of energies?

Akhira: Yes, we sit together in a garden, but we don't have to tell her our experiences, or about our practices because she has done that and she knows exactly what we're feeling.

Joanna: How many are in this group being trained?

Akhira: Four. I'm the youngest and I make five. In Alexandria, I am the last to be prepared to complete the group. This training is important for the group.

Joanna: Did Mother Mary come to visit your group?

Akhira: She was in charge of us, not always there, but she was supervising everyone. She came to see that everything was all right.

Joanna: Was your family in contact with Mary Magdalene and Mother Mary?

Akhira: Yes, they knew all of us in the community. When I was chosen for the training, everyone in the community knew what it was all about, and my parents knew.

Joanna: So it was an honor for your family?

Akhira: Yes, it was something very special.

Joanna: Were you one of Jeshua's female disciples?

Akhira: Yes, I was one of the group of Mary Magdalene.

Joanna: How did you perceive the difference between the two Marys: Mary Magdalene and Mother Mary?

Akhira : Mary Magdalene is more loving, more relaxed. Mother Mary is more serious, she has a bigger responsibility. Mary Magdalene is natural and loving and relaxed.

Joanna: Did you sense that Mother Mary and Mary Magdalene were working as part of a team?

Akhira: Yes, they work as part of the team, but they're different. Each has her role...each has her own task and they are preparing us.

Joanna: And Mary Magdalene is ten years or so older than you?

Akhira: Yes, between ten and fifteen years older ...

Joanna: So your training, it took how long?

Akhira: The training in Alexandria was the final period of instruction. I had been trained before in Israel, and then I went to Alexandria and that was the final training before this ceremony. And later I went with Benjamin back to a community in Israel and we stayed there.

Joanna: The ceremony, was it an Isis initiation in Alexandria?

Akhira: Yes, I saw golden pyramids, and a big gold triangle. Couldn't see all round me during the ceremony...I was lying on a bed shaped like a pyramid, with the top cut off it, so it had high sides. And there was a priestess conducting the ceremony, and behind me there were golden Egyptian carved figures.

Joanna: Would Mary Magdalene have gone through a ceremony like this too?

Akhira: Yes, she had the same training as we had.

Joanna: But Mother Mary had come through a different training?

Akhira: She had gone through a similar training too, but it was not here at Alexandria. I feel closer to Mary Magdalene than to Mother Mary...maybe it's because Mother Mary is older. Mary Magdalene is our confidante, she shares the same knowledge ...she is like a big sister.

Comment by Stuart: What emerges from this is the warm and affectionate side of Mary Magdalene when she was with groups of women training in the same Isis tradition. The answer to the question about female disciples was particularly interesting. We shall return to the female disciples of Jeshua later, but here Akhira is saying that some of these disciples were being taught and guided by Mary Magdalene. In delegating the role of Teacher and Mentor in this way, Jeshua was acknowledging that Mary Magdalene was advanced enough to have disciples of her own, something that puts her into quite a new context as a Teacher of major stature. This information is important because it goes so far beyond what we have in the biblical record, and starts to build up a much more impressive picture of Mary Magdalene as a high Initiate.

During March 2007, Isabel and Michael returned for a second session with us. After Isabel was taken back to her life as Akhira, Joanna asked her to explore the knowledge she had at that time through her contact with Mary Magdalene.

Akhira: So much love, so much love. Such a close relationship. It's like coming home.

The energy connection with Mary Magdalene was so powerful for Isabel at this point that she needed to pause and breathe deeply before she could continue.

Akhira: I feel Mary Magdalene, I feel her energy, I feel her closeness, I feel at home. We're always connected, but now we're together.
Joanna: She was your major teacher, wasn't she?
Akhira: Yes. We loved each other so much, we were so close. . . we were always together.

Joanna: Were you together from a very early age?

Akhira: Yes, she was my teacher, my sister, my friend. We were such a strong team, such a close team.

Joanna: Yes. and you had to be, didn't you?

Akhira: Yes.

Joanna: Who were you named after as Akhira?

Akhira: They call me "princess".

Stuart: Then perhaps "Akhira" was the name of a princess.

Akhira: They call me "princess," that's true.

Comment by Stuart: In the modern world, it is unusual for any country to have more than one royal family, but the situation in Israel two thousand years ago was quite different. During that period, the leaders of several of the tribes tried to maintain some outward signs of royal or quasi-royal status. Hence, in the Israel of that time, the title "princess" was more widely used than its modern equivalent in Europe.

The session continues:

Joanna: I feel the people around you really looked up to you...they recognized your Light.

Akhira: I'm still a child at this point ...everybody loves me. It's so easy. Everybody loves me and I love everybody. It's total joy, total happiness, total peace. Yes, they call me "little princess". Our lives are not all ceremonial, they enjoy life and play with me.

Joanna: How old were you when you went to the place of learning?

Akhira: I was small when I went there.

Joanna: What do you need to learn?

Akhira: I need to learn the ceremonies. I have to learn to do the ceremonies with the others, how to present it. It's like choreography. I have to learn the outer things of the ceremonies, how to do it, how to prepare, who does what...the steps I take, and the clothes I wear.

Joanna: So would you like to talk about one of the ceremonies and what you wear?

Akhira: I have this ...golden hair to put on, and a golden robe, and I carry a box.

Joanna: What's in the box?

Akhira: It's closed. The shape of the lid is like the roof of a house, and it's golden with some decorations. During the ceremony, people will open it and take something out. But now I'm rehearsing and I don't know what's inside the box. They're training me in how to carry the box.

Joanna: Let's go a little forward to the point where you find out what's in the box.

Akhira: It's gold powder, and during the ceremony the priests eat some. The ceremony consecrates the powder and then each priest gets some. They are all in the same kind of clothes that I have, made out of golden cloth, and gold on their heads. The women have special make-up on their faces and everybody looks beautiful.

Joanna: I understand that etherium gold was used to expand the consciousness...

Akhira: Yes. There were three kinds of this gold.

Comment by Stuart: Etherium Gold (also called Monatomic Gold) is a trace mineral that occurs naturally in ancient mineral deposits. It takes the form of a powder with unusual electromagnetic and superconductive properties. Etherium Gold is also reputed to have remarkable abilities to release energies at the cellular level, energise the body and transform the DNA. Ancient Egyptian texts talk of using "white powder of gold" to nourish the Light Body.

The session continues:

Joanna: And what was Michael's role at that time?

60

Akhira: He was one of those who organized the ceremony.
Joanna: You said there were three kinds of gold – could you tell us about that?

Akhira: In this moment, in this ceremony, I don't take it. I just bring it to the others. The young girls and the priestesses take the white-gold powder. There is also a more brown powder and a more golden one. All the young ones take the white one.

During this session, Michael had been tuning in to this shared life and he was able to add some detail at this point.

Michael: It was the educational level. The first one was to sustain the body and ground it. The second powder was to connect with the Light and happiness.
Joanna: So the brown powder connected you with joy?
Michael: And the third golden one was for release.
Akhira: The men on the left side, they take the brown one.
Joanna: So you have to step up the frequencies until you get more advanced, starting with the white powder and moving on eventually to the gold one?
Akhira. Yes. I take the gold one, but not in the ceremony. If it's a ceremony for me only, I take it, the golden one.
Joanna: And this is when you're a little bit older?
Akhira: Yes, when I'm eleven or twelve.
Joanna: So when you were younger, you took the white powder and graduated to the gold one?
Akhira: Yes. I take it regularly in a ceremony only for myself, maybe weekly. I don't know exactly what it does – they don't tell me everything.
Joanna: Can you imagine you've taken some of the golden powder – what has happened?
Akhira: I take a teaspoon of powder and dissolve it in my mouth. It's energy, it's holding the body, it goes into the head.

Joanna: My sense is that it's clearing the energy so you can remain as light and pure as possible.

Akhira: Yes. *It releases blockages all over the body. Then the body feels like golden light, like the Light Body, very strong and golden. And it lasts, it's meant to last all day, to keep the energies charged.*

We were able to ask Alariel (in a separate session) about the use at that time of Etherium Gold, and this was his response:

Alariel: Etherium Gold was valued throughout the Mystery Schools of the Middle East, but it was in Egypt that it was used with the greatest understanding and precision. A whole technology surrounding its use developed within the Egyptian Mystery School tradition, and that use was carefully controlled. The Egyptians saw it primarily as a means of strengthening the link with the Light Body, also called the Merkabah: this is the vehicle of ascension. But as a prelude to this work, it also acted to purify the subtle levels within the body-mind link. This was a key to passing safely and swiftly through the process of enlightenment and ascension. In this way, it became a vital tool supporting the whole work of accelerating and uplifting human consciousness.

Comment by Stuart: Ascension is an advanced stage of human evolution, in which the aspirant raises his or her vibration and merges with the Light.

The session continues:

Akhira: It is in the future that I will do what my mission is, but at the moment, I'm living here with all these wonderful people and doing the ceremonies with the powder.

Joanna: Do you have any sense of what your mission is yet?

Akhira: I have the power of doing things. They know it will be very important. They are preparing me for this. I see the image of another ceremony, and there I am standing very decorated and with something large and golden around the head. This time I am presiding in the ceremony like a priest, and they bring offerings, food and incense and candles and gold. When they bring this to me, they are asking me, or asking the universe through me, that something can be done. I can bring information through and do ceremonies and I do some signs with my hands. I'm doing a language with my hands and talking to them on a telepathic level, giving information and giving instructions. And there is an information beam through my third eye. It's a ceremony that takes place regularly. Everybody here is very advanced; it's all priests and priestesses.

Joanna: So what's the purpose of all this telepathic communication? Are you preparing for something?

Akhira: Yes, we are preparing and I'm giving instructions saying what needs to be done and exactly what's going to happen. It's something very special that will involve all of us working together. I'm soon going to leave here, and I'm leaving them with instructions. I'm traveling to where it's going to happen. I'm not staying in this temple. This will be the last time I talk to them today. Everybody is very well prepared. A very strong team.

Joanna: What is your mission in this new place?

Akhira: I have to stay very close to what is going to happen. Carry an energy inside me that needs to be present. It's one part of the process that the energy I carry needs to be there. I'm supporting what's going to happen.

Joanna: So what is happening?

Akhira: Mary Magdalene knows that, but I just carry this energy and that is going to help her.

Joanna: She needs the support of a team because she has a big job ahead of her?

Akhira: Yes. She and Jeshua have to do this. I am in different clothes already, and we are in Israel. I stay most of the time with Mary Magdalene. I am her support, her assistant. I am holding her energy, recharging her and on the outer side helping her with all kinds of other things. But it's not really the outer work I do that is important, it's the inner work. I'm always with her, we go here and there together. She meets with different people all the time, she's very busy, and she 's nervous.

Joanna: Because she knows she's taken on a big job?

Akhira: Yes. We go to these meetings, just the two of us. She's talking to different people and I go with her.

Joanna: Do you remember her first meeting with Jeshua? Did they grow up as children together?

Akhira: Yes. They were meant to be together...they recognized each other. He knew, Mary knew, Mother Mary knew, I knew. The other group, the apostles, didn't understand everything. They were on a different level.

Joanna: Because they had to do more of the outer work?

Akhira: Yes.

Comment by Stuart: Our next question focuses on the Core Group, a secret inner group within the Essene Brotherhood which supported the work of Jeshua. There is a chapter on the Core Group in our first book.

Joanna: I understand that the Core Group held a lot of the knowledge, and it's like circles going out. The further you are from the Core Group, the less knowledge you would have.

Akhira: The Core Group had a very strong energy.

Joanna: And that energy radiated out?

Akhira: Yes, it's like a fractal, an energy field going out and interacting all together. It's very complex levels of energy, fields of energy that have geometrical patterns so that all the levels interact all with each other, layers of different patterns.

Joanna: So it's essential that all the layers are functioning?

Akhira: Yes, you can't take one layer away. This whole system is like a geometrical pattern, so if you take a piece out it wouldn't be complete any more.

Joanna: It's holographic isn't it?

Akhira: Yes, and the energetic fields which have geometrical patterns are not only in the third dimension.

Stuart: They are multidimensional?

Akhira: It's in all dimensions but they interact and this creates a huge energy that is there in these groups and all their work.

Stuart: So it's a complete energy system?

Akhira: Yes, on many levels.

Joanna: So it's like a lattice-work?

Akhira: Yes, exactly like a lattice ...If you see it from the outside, it feeds into all different directions and dimensions.

Joanna: A holographic web?

Akhira: A holographic spider's web, exactly. And the fields make patterns in greens, blues, violets, so you can see the shape. They are not solid, they are energy fields, but you can still see the shape and they have different textures of blues, and a little bit metallic, iridescent and crystalline. It's a system on its own, almost a universe on its own.

Stuart: What is feeding through this system, is it energy, or information?

Akhira: Most of it is information. The interaction is mostly information. It's patterns, it's information.

Joanna: So much of the information is contained in the pattern which the person picks up telepathically?

Akhira: Yes, the groups meet, but much of the work is done telepathically.

Joanna: So these lines are used to send telepathic signals?

Akhira: Yes. It's a system that's working well.

Joanna: A language of Light which will come back to our planet for us to remember.

Akhira: Yes, a remembering and keeping this knowledge alive because that is all linked in with the telepathic ability. The system gives information about logistics and organization, but it's the knowledge which interacts. And this is due to their having some part of their consciousness activated. Because of this activation, they can be in contact with each other, and have access to many things which other humans don't have.

Joanna: So it's a very sophisticated kind of network, a purer network than many of the esoteric schools at that time were able to connect into?

Akhira: To tune in, you had to be on the same level, using the same intuition and having the same codes. If you don't have this level of encodement, you can't connect in.

At this point in the session something quite extraordinary happened. Akhira began to talk in an ancient language, very different from random speech because it contained repeating patterns and specific rhythms.

Joanna: Can you tell us about this language? Does it have a name?

Akhira: It's a language used in Atlantis.

Joanna: Has it come down in its original form to the time now when you know it as Akhira, or had it changed by then?

Akhira: It was a secret language by then. It was not widely used then, but certain people knew it. It was only the initiates who used this language. The vibrational power of language is very important. We did communicate telepathically, but the words had a strong vibration, so during ceremonies it was important that the words were spoken out, and this vibration was released.

Joanna: So in remembering this knowledge, the language can come back and bring its vibration?

Akhira: The vibration of the words themselves can heal at a deep level, and can release blockages deep within us. So this language is healing at a very profound level. Just the vibration releases blockages.

After the session when Isabel was still in the energy of that life, she said that what Akhira was trying to say was that the vibration of this language can heal the DNA, and release blockages in the DNA.

Joanna: So this secret language is part of the knowledge that you had at the time of Jeshua?

Isabel: Yes, it's one part, but there is more wisdom from that time that we can access. There is much work to do, but we need to heal ourselves. Dissonant frequencies hold magnetic fields that are lower-vibrating and these hold all our pain and suffering and all our illnesses. We need to bring in the higher-vibrating harmonic fields to create a new reality. We have been hiding this secret language and the secret knowledge for so long and it needs to be released to do the work that needs to be done now.

Comment by Stuart: This had been a remarkable session of very high energy, and it had opened up information on a very subtle level. Akhira's devotion and dedication to Mary Magdalene shines through her account. This is the real story of Mary Magdalene, not the distorted version put out by the early Church Fathers, who clearly had a powerful agenda and an absolute determination that women should never have leading roles in the Christian Church. History has not dealt kindly with these prelates of the early Church, and their reputation steadily diminishes while that of Mary Magdalene grows ever stronger.

One of the most interesting things about this second session with Isabel is how much it advances the story, adding many new layers of understanding about Akhira, Mary Magdalene, and the life they shared together. The information on the ancient and powerful language was also a great gift. Any knowledge that offers the possibility of healing the DNA surely deserves our attention at a time when the journey towards wholeness is so important.

We noticed that the language was described as being "used in Atlantis" which suggests that this was not an Atlantean language as such, but something much older. Several ancient civilizations preserved older languages for ceremonial use, so that they were only spoken by priests or priestesses, and perhaps this is an example of that practice.

8

Laura Clare

In the summer of 2006 Emma, a past life therapist living in the Lyme Bay area in the West of England, contacted Joanna asking to do a past life session with her. Emma felt a connection with the time and place described in our book, and the induction took her back to a life in Israel two thousand years ago.

Emma saw herself as a girl about ten with long, slim, brown legs and bare feet. She was feeling a little wild as if she had been running. She saw herself in front of a white archway.

Later in this session we established that her name in this life was Laura Clare. The tradition of giving two names leads to a degree of flexibility as to whether one or the other name is emphasized, or both are used together. Emma's account makes it clear that "Laura" was the preferred name within the family, whilst Daniel's reference to her in *The Essenes, Children of the Light* shows that "Clare" was used in wider Essene circles outside the immediate family. Now that we have identified Laura, we will use that name from this point on.

Laura: I feel the wind in my long hair as I get to this building. There's someone here that I have got to give a message to. I'm out of breath from all this running...there's a sense of excitement...I'm proud of my mission. I have got to tell this person, and I have a feeling I'm not normally supposed to go into this place. I want to go in...there are lots of people and many of them are dressed in white. They're bigger than me and I go nipping between them, darting about, and I'm little so if someone tries to grab me and stop me, I've gone before they can get me.

Joanna: Because your mission is too important and nobody's going to stop you, are they?

Laura: No.

Joanna: Are you heading for one particular person?

Laura: My brother. I have a message for my brother, and no one's going to stop me till I get to him. And he's important, or so I'm told. When he comes home, lots of people come and it's nice.

Laura never names her brother as Jeshua, and he is always referred to simply as "my brother". However, her account taken as a whole makes it quite clear that Jeshua was her brother.

Joanna: Do you know what's contained in this message for your brother?

Laura: He has to come, somebody's ill. He has to come quick. They're trying to stop me, but I have got to...

Joanna: Have you managed to get to him?

Laura: I've told someone I recognize and he's telling him. And he's coming and then I'm running out.

Joanna: Are you very close to your brother?

Laura: Yes.

Joanna: So this is why it's so important; you know he's the one person who can help. So you're running ahead to tell them he's on his way.

Laura: They're coming, they're all running because they know it's important. I don't want to go in the house, I don't want to see.

Joanna: Is it your mother who is ill?

Laura: No, it's a young man, a cousin. Now my brother's come out and he's done the work to make him better. Then I come and sit in the garden that slopes away from the house. I have a dog I can talk to, and I keep telling him that he'll make him well.

Joanna: Would you like to talk a little about your brother?

Laura: He's a teacher and he has many followers and he's just lovely.

Joanna: Is he an older brother?

Laura: Yes.

Joanna: Are there many in your family?

Laura: There are other brothers, but he's special.

Joanna: The one you're closest to?

Laura: I wouldn't say close because I'm little and he's important, but he does love me and when he can, he spends time with me. I know him, I know he's good. He's here to do something important, and he does. He made someone see who couldn't, he's so clever.

Joanna: It must be wonderful to have a brother like that.

Laura: Yes, he's lovely and everybody talks about him. Wherever you go, they're talking about my brother.

Joanna: Do you want to tell me about your family and your mother?

Laura: My mother's lovely, she's very calm and gentle.

Joanna: Are you part of a community?

Laura: We have a house, and I can go in different houses because they all know me.

Joanna: Is that unusual for a girl at this time?

Laura: I'm a bit wild...I would say I was special. I know I'm lucky, I'm special. Not everybody has a brother like my brother.

Joanna: But though he's special, it must be quite difficult to share him with others.

Laura: He was away when I was little and then he came back. We always talked about him and I knew he was special, he was a teacher. It's lovely at the moment because he's at home quite a lot, more than ever before. And I hope he stays here.

We're always cooking and I help because there's always lots of people. Joanna: Do you go to school?

Laura: I study...I'm learning to write, but not many girls do. I want to know about all sorts of things. I want to know about the things that grow that you can take when you're ill and that's what my brother does. He knows what to give people and what to do, and I want to learn that. Plants are my friends and I want to know more about them so I'm studying them. When I'm with the flowers, they talk to me...if you know what a flower is, they will talk back.

Joanna: It's as if you tune in to them?

Laura: They can talk, but only if you know... I know that they know me.

Joanna: You recognize each other.

Laura: Yes, that's right. And I love it that I'm so little and I can sit at the level of the flowers, and sit under the bushes and look up at them. I love it, I hide there. It started when I was playing when I was little. I would go and hide in the bush and the bush would talk to me. There is a nice lady who is my teacher, but now she knows that I know quite a lot.

Joanna: So you have a responsible position for a very young girl.

Laura: Not all the teachers can talk as I can, and sometimes the teachers ask me to ask the plants. I think I'm very lucky.

Joanna: Are the plants your main area of interest?

Laura: The flowers and the trees. The trees I want to climb, I like to get up to the top and no one can see me and then the trees talk to me.

Joanna: It sounds like a very happy life.

Laura: It's lovely, and when I get big I want to be a teacher like my brother and I want to make people better. I can go out and call the flowers and say, "Who will help with this?" Someone had spots on their body and one of the flowers said, "Take me and squeeze me and put me on the spots." I did, and the spots got better.

Joanna: It's a wonderful gift to be able to do that.

Laura: I'm only ten now, but they tell me that to do this, I must have studied it before.

Joanna: That was good that they recognized you had a real gift.

Laura: I know that I'm lucky, but there was another time when I was a little girl when it wasn't all like this. This is a very special time for me because I'm in this protected place with these wonderful people who let me be a wild child, I'm not restricted. If I want to sleep under the stars I can...it's lovely. My brother's here now so no one will notice me, and I can spend more time in the garden. They're all very busy because he's important and they have all these people coming and they're so busy that they don't notice me.

Joanna: Do you want to tell me about the healings he does? Does he work with the energies in his hands?

Laura: Yes, he works with whatever we have in our house...different pots of herbs we've made up and it's written on them what they can do. People come to the house because they know about us.

Joanna: So there's a group of you doing this?

Laura: Well, you could say my family is special, and my brother's special. It seems that we've known all this for a very long time, we are a group of people who know many things. There's a story that we are from a very old time, an old place where everybody knew all this. And now it seems that in the world there's not many people who know this any more. We have to keep this knowledge because there might not be many people like me later, and it's terribly important that we keep this knowledge. It's our family's job to keep this knowledge.

Joanna: So you are the keepers of ancient secrets?

Laura: Yes. Other people know things about sound, about music. I like music, but I don't know about it. They can do things, they can heal with a sound, and it's amazing what these people know. I wish I could live forever and then I could learn all this.

Joanna: Do you want to talk about other skills your people have like healing with the hands?

Laura: The people now, they don't know what people really are, they think people are just the body. We know that God is in us, and it comes out of us if we choose to use it. If you choose to use the hand, the God-energy will come out of the hands. But we can use it through our eyes or through the mouth when we talk and make people better. I think everyone has this God-energy, but they don't know it. We know it and teach our children. It's our job to pass on this information.

Joanna: Is there anything else you want to tell me about this time when you are ten?

Laura: It's the most wonderful life. I just want it to go on. It's lovely with my brother having time at home with us, and because he's home, I can spend more time with my plants in the garden. There's never a night when there aren't people in the house, so I can do what I want.

Joanna: Has your brother been traveling somewhere?

Laura: He was away when I was little. Then I didn't really see him.

Joanna: Did he ever talk about his travels?

Laura: He went a long, long way across the sea. He's been in many boats, and gone away to see people who were his teachers.

Joanna: Do you know whose boats he went in?

Laura: Yes, they belonged to Joseph, my uncle. I don't see him very much, he's very important and he travels. He took my brother away to study, but I study here in the garden.

Comment by Stuart: The person referred to here is Joseph of Arimathea, one of the main characters in our book *The Essenes, Children of the Light.*

The session continues:

74

Joanna: Is your uncle Joseph a good friend of your father?

Laura: Of my mother, I think. When he is here, I don't get to see my mother because she loves her brother like I love my brother. I'm so lucky.

Joanna: Your father is also called Joseph. Is he still alive?

Laura : No.

Joanna: So this is why your uncle Joseph comes, he's taken responsibility for your family?

Laura: I suppose so. He certainly looks after my brother a lot...I don't want the grownups fussing about me. I don't mind when they go away.

Joanna: Would you like to move forward now to the next big event that happens in your life?

Laura: It's difficult because I think it's not good. ..I don't want to grow up...

Joanna: It's been really idyllic and I think you have a sense that it's not going to be as good when you get older.

Laura: No, it's not...I don't want to look at it...I want to jump a lot of years ...I want to be really grown up.

Joanna: What age are you now?

Laura: I've jumped twenty years. I'm now thirty...it doesn't feel the same. I think I've gone across the sea on one of those ships.

Joanna: Do you know who the owner of the ship is?

Laura: It's a Joseph ship...I don't even want to think about getting here, it was a bad time.

Joanna: Have you now gone to a new country?

Laura: It's not my country. It's hard now...the flowers are different...I try to make sense of it all.

Joanna: Of what's happened?

Laura: Yes. Before, when I was little, the flowers talked to me, and it seems in this land, flowers aren't used to talking...Maybe I have to wake the flowers up here. This is a very strange place...it's heavy. And I'm heavy because I'm wearing a coat, and I never wore a coat before. I'm in a cold place, but I have to keep on with the teaching. I was all right when I was little. It's as if I had a premonition, when I was a child, that it ...wasn't going to last. And it didn't. And we have come here and I have to keep this knowledge and I have a child. I have a daughter, and I have to teach her. She's a sweet little thing. I call her Laura, too...And I have a husband.

Joanna: Was he from your community?

Laura: He came with us on the boat. We didn't stay in the first country, some of our people did, but we didn't. It was a very long journey. We had to go to where my brother had been with my uncle...I am so tired. The trees don't talk to me and in my own country they talk to me...It 's so hard here.

Joanna: Are there any people from this new country who can help you?

Laura: They knew us and were expecting us.

Joanna: What do these people call your brother?

Laura: Savior...it's so long and so weary. I have a beloved husband, his name is James...I am so tired and I have so much to do. We have to start a community here. I live near the sea and love the sea.

Joanna: Is this place in Gaul?

Laura: That was where we went through. Now we've come here to the sacred isle.

Joanna: Is this something to do with Avalon?

Laura: Our community is there, but I stayed here by the sea because I was too sick. I was going to Avalon...but was too sick to get there. I stayed by the sea...I don't know if the trees here will talk to me...the plants are so different here. My daughter is about five now. We sit in the garden, but I'm still very weak.

Comment by Stuart: The Isle of Avalon was the original name for the place in Somerset in the West of England which is now called Glastonbury.

The session continues:

Joanna: Does Laura look like any members of your family?

Laura: She has the eyes of my brother. She is a special child, and if only I wasn't so weary, I could teach her.

Joanna: And she probably has natural gifts of her own.

Laura: She sings. She healed me with her singing. My mother sang. I didn't sing so much.

Joanna: And did her mother before her sing too?

Laura: Yes. She sang in a tongue which is not our own...an ancient language which heals. I don't speak that language, I speak the language of the flowers.

Joanna: But even if you don't speak a language, you can benefit from it.

Laura: I can, it is wonderful. You are transported...I think I go back to the old lands when she sings. I see these amazing temples...and fantastic golden buildings, and I seem to be rising up with the angels when she sings. And I know that everything has not been lost, nothing has been lost. When she sings, she holds the memory of that ancient time when we all knew who we were. And we were all whole...and little Laura has come in with this gift. But I'm still worried about my gift which isn't good in this country. I can't seem to get these plants to talk as they did in my homeland.

Joanna: Perhaps that won't happen till you're feeling a bit better.

Laura: My husband is a fisherman and he brings fish for us. These people here are very kind to us and they have children who play with my daughter.

Joanna: I feel much of your illness may be connected with the sadness of what you've left behind.

Laura: I was with him when they took him down... I was there. And we brought him back to life...we did, we did! The plants spoke so much that night, the plants had never spoken so much. They called to me and told me what to do. And we worked and we worked and healed that wound.

Joanna: You didn't have much chance to express how you felt because you had a job to do and you had to get on with it.

Laura: *I put a flower in the wound* (sobs and expresses deep emotion).

Joanna: You need to express these feelings if you're able to, and then they are gone, and they don't need to haunt you any longer. You did such a good job that night, such a good job.

Laura: *The wound grew over the flower. The wound grew over the flower! The flowers were telling me what to do and I told the others. We did it. But he was different, he was of God...he was special.*

Joanna: So was your mother.

Laura: *She was.*

Joanna: It must have been such an ordeal for her, and it was a major feat to heal your brother – that was what your training was preparing you for.

Laura: *This is why now these flowers don't speak to me. I didn't understand that before...oh, my heart hurts. It was those flowers that had to heal him. I left that other country because I didn't like its flowers. But now I see that the whole flower healing was for that end – we did it. Here in this country, the flowers don't speak because they don't have to.*

Joanna: It really took it out of you in the tomb.

Laura: *I have been a little sick since then.*

Joanna: It was such an achievement.

Laura: *My husband is good. He cares for me and he cares for my daughter.*

Joanna: It was such a big achievement. No one was sure whether you would bring it off. But you knew you had a mission and there was something important you had to do.

Laura: *The flowers spoke to me and told me what to do. When it was clear that they wanted to kill my brother, I knew from the flowers that I would be allowed to make him better. The flowers told me, so I was prepared. I was young, about thirteen years old, but all the people knew I had a gift of the flowers. And because of my unusual childhood, they allowed me to tell them what to do. The wound was my biggest challenge...the bleeding was such that he would have died. The flower had to be put there very quickly. More than that, the connection with his breathing. We had to put some flowers in his nose and his mouth so that the perfume would trigger the breathing again. Some of the stronger men were massaging his heart. My main concentration was on the flowers in the wound to close the wound.*

Joanna: Was Luke there with his crystals?

Laura: When I put the flowers in the wound, I think lavender helped with the healing. Then crystals were used on his head and on his throat, and to trigger energy in the third eye and the throat and the solar plexus. The people with the crystals had them underneath him and on top of him, pointing towards his spine. I had to work with the flowers in the wound. Flowers would talk to me...it was an amazing thing to see.

Joanna: It's an incredible thing to do. Do you want to tell me more about that time?

Laura: I became weak and I went to sleep in the garden and later I was taken home because I was ill. And then within a short time my mother and brothers and I were told we must go. And my uncle had prepared for this, the same as my uncle prepared for everything. Uncle Joseph was a powerful person and because he knew what was happening, he could plan in advance. And so it was arranged that we would leave.

Joanna: You left so much behind, but you had to leave it behind.

Laura: My brother is alive – it worked! We knew that, but many of his followers didn't know...but I was weak and ill by then. I remember being carried from the house at night ...and then being carried down to go on the boat. I think I had a high temperature by then. I only began to get well on the boat. And then I began to love the sea and the song of the sea, and my mother would sing to me as she used to sing. My mother is a wonderful, wonderful being. She is in the Isle of Avalon, but I can't get there at the moment because I'm sick. But we did it, we fulfilled our prophecy, we did what we had to do.

Joanna: Did you ever get to the Isle of Avalon?

Laura: I was taken to the Isle of Avalon, but by then I preferred to live by the sea, it suited me. That beautiful bay, that beautiful hill. I lived there. I loved that place and I stayed there. I visited my mother when I was a little better.

Joanna: Was she still on the Isle of Avalon?

Laura: She was, yes. And they had a big community there. We had a small one here by the sea.

Comment by Stuart: It seems likely that Laura Clare lived near Lyme Bay in Dorset. This would have been near one of the routes which were used for moving tin from Cornwall to northern Gaul. Emma had clearly felt a strong connection with this area and has chosen to live there in this present life. We often find that people feel strongly drawn to areas where they had experienced a powerful or significant past life.

The session continues:

Joanna: In the area of Avalon where you were I understand they had an oral tradition, but they also imprinted the knowledge within the stones.

Laura: In the same way as I talk to the flowers and the flowers talk to me, those ancient people spoke to the stones and the stones spoke to them. These Druid people knew the stone was as much a golden being as a person. And they could talk to the stones and that is how they could get the stones to move to the shape they wanted.

Joanna: Did your brother ever get married?

Laura: My brother had his beautiful bride, Mary. And Mary taught us all so much because Mary and my brother were an

80

equal couple and this was unusual, and we learnt how to be a man and woman equal, like a right hand and left hand balancing each other, both equally important. We learnt from them, they were the perfect pair, they were our teachers. And by being with them, we learnt many things.

Joanna: Because many things are learned just by being with special people.

Laura: Yes, and I could ask Mary. I could go to her and tell her if I had a problem.

Joanna: So Mary would have been a bit older than you?

Laura: Yes, I was much younger.

Joanna: I'm getting the picture of you having a special place in her heart.

Laura: She was my teacher.

Joanna: Did you know where Mary originally had her training?

Laura: Mary had her teachers, the Egyptian priestesses. She and I knew each other in a previous time in Egypt. This is why she recognized me as a child and taught me many things. Our family was Jewish, but I had been Egyptian in a previous life. She was trained from a small girl to fulfill her prophecy. She was a wonderful being. She had been my High Priestess in that life before in Egypt, parts of which at times I would remember, and I would remember her and how wonderful she was. And in that life, she was my teacher also.

We were very fortunate to be able to explore this life and add more detail to the brief glimpse of Clare in *The Essenes, Children of the Light*. Here she emerges as a strong personality in her own right, even as a ten-year-old. And the passages focusing on her training in the use of flowers and herbs help to explain how she was able to develop a high level of expertise and become a key figure in the process of healing Jeshua in the tomb. Through her account, we also get some idea of life in the household run by Mary Anna, a household which moved into a much higher level of activity whenever Jeshua came to stay.

During this session we were not sure which flower had been used to close up the wound, but the morning after the session Emma phoned Joanna in a very excited state. She told her how she had awoken early with the memory that somewhere in her collection she had a book on the flowers of this region. When she found it, this book turned out to be *Wild Flowers of the Holy Land* by the renowned Israeli naturalist Uzi Paz. Flicking through the pages, Emma discovered the daisy-like flower she had seen in her session. It blooms in the spring and its Latin name is *Calendula Palaestina*. As she excitedly told Joanna, "I healed the wound with Calendula – just as I might heal a wound today!" To Emma this discovery was a real confirmation of the validity of what she had experienced during the regression process the previous day.

Laura's story is a remarkable one, and it sheds light on so many areas, not least of which is the healing process in the tomb and Jeshua's recovery after the crucifixion, which we touched on in *The Essenes, Children of the Light*. The responsibility of being one of the leaders in the team which healed Jeshua bore down heavily on the thirteen-year-old Laura, and she paid a heavy price in the ill health she experienced during her life as an adult. Yet taken as a whole, this life has a very positive feeling about it because her early experiences as Jeshua's sister were so powerful and significant.

9

The Female Disciples

During another session with Alariel, some very important – long-hidden information came to light.

Joanna: We understand that there were a number of female disciples of Jeshua in addition to the traditional list of twelve male disciples given in the Bible. How many disciples of Jeshua were there in total?

Alariel: It's important to understand that the discipleship system that Jeshua set up was designed to mirror the greater symbolism of the Universe. The balance of Father-Mother God was mirrored in a balance of male and female disciples. So there were six circles of twelve, making 72 male disciples, and six circles of twelve, making 72 female disciples – a total of 144 disciples in all. The names of the first circle of twelve male disciples have come down to you and are well attested. However much less is known about the first circle of female disciples, and we can now talk about that. First of all we have two advanced initiates who were frankly head and shoulders above the rest, and these were Mary Anna, the mother of Jeshua, and Mary Magdalene. These were initiates who had reached high levels of spiritual attainment long before that time. They arrived in Israel as fully qualified adepts, both very advanced in their own way. So they were head and shoulders above the rest of the group and were respected as such.

Comment by Stuart: An *adept* is a term for a high Initiate, a Sage or Master-soul.

The session continues:

Alariel: Then you have Helena Salome, who took the matronymic name of Mary. Outside the family group she was often called Mary Salome. She was the sister of Mary Anna, and therefore an aunt of Jeshua. In the biblical account of the crucifixion, she is simply called Salome. She married Lazarus, also called Zebedee, and her sons John and James were disciples.

Mary Anna's sister Mary Jacoby, an aunt of Jeshua, was a disciple. She married Clopas, also called Cleophas, and their daughter Abigail was a disciple; she married the disciple John.

Martha of Bethany was a disciple; she was a sister of Lazarus.

Martha's sister Mary was a disciple.

Mary Anna had a sister called Rebekah and her daughter Mariam Joanna, a cousin of Jeshua, was a disciple.

Mary Anna's brother Isaac had a daughter called Sara, a cousin of Jeshua, and she was a disciple; she married the disciple Philip.

Laura Clare, also called Ruth, a sister of Jeshua was a disciple. Although Greek names were popular at that time (examples being Helena and Philip), Latin names were rarely used because of the unpopularity of the Roman occupation. The name "Laura Clare" is an exception to this, and came about because Joseph of Arimathea had a great friend amongst the senior Roman administrators whose wife was called Laura Clare. Through her brother Joseph, Mary met Laura Clare and became her friend, being able to see beyond the prejudice of the time and recognize her soul qualities. Mary named her daughter after this wise and beautiful Roman lady, but also gave her the Hebrew name of Ruth, so that she could use that name outside the extended family.

Lois Salome, a daughter of Joseph of Arimathea and a cousin of Jeshua, was a disciple.

Susannah Mary, a daughter of Joseph of Arimathea and a cousin of Jeshua, was a disciple.

That is the full list of the twelve first circle female disciples.

Comment by Stuart: what emerges clearly from this list is that everyone on it was related to Jeshua, either directly or through marriage. It is a fascinating list and we summarize it here:

1   Mary Anna, the mother of Jeshua.
2   Mary Magdalene, the spiritual partner of Jeshua.
3   Helena Salome, an aunt of Jeshua and the wife of Lazarus.
4   Mary Jacoby, an aunt of Jeshua and the wife of Clopas.
5   Abigail their daughter, a cousin of Jeshua.
6   Martha of Bethany, a sister of Lazarus.
7   Mary, the sister of Martha.
8   Mariam Joanna, a cousin of Jeshua.
9   Sara, a cousin of Jeshua.
10 Laura Clare, a sister of Jeshua.
11 Lois Salome, a cousin of Jeshua.
12 Susannah Mary, a cousin of Jeshua.

The session continues:

Joanna: It must have been very difficult for the female disciples to give as much time to Jeshua as they would have liked if they had families to look after.

Alariel: The second circle of female disciples were enormously supportive of the first circle, and they provided support in covering family and community duties which made it possible for the first circle to spend much of their time with Jeshua. Jeshua regarded the help and generous, open-hearted sharing amongst the female disciples as a model of Unconditional Love, and brought this to the attention of the male disciples, amongst whom it was not widely understood or very well received. The male disciples regarded themselves as teachers and leaders, and saw the role of women as listening and following. So it was hard for them to accept that the females had anything at all to teach them.

As Jeshua put Unconditional Love at the very center of his teaching, this made it all the more irritating to the men, who would have preferred he had taught some more intellectual or philosophical doctrine based upon reason rather than upon heart-energy. They felt ill at ease in matters of heart-energy, and longed to elaborate or structuralize Jeshua's teaching in some way, to make it more intellectually challenging and therefore more impressive to the male mind. They saw heart-energy as much too vague and insubstantial, and longed for a set of logical and profound concepts that would seize the high ground of intellectual debate. They saw Jeshua's great intellectual gifts in debating (especially in his debates with the Pharisees he encountered), but they couldn't understand why he should have chosen so flimsy a foundation for his teaching as Unconditional Love.

Comment by Stuart: The Pharisees were the rabbinic group within Judaism which controlled the education process in the synagogues.

The session continues:

Alariel: Of course they dared not raise these questions while Jeshua was teaching them, for he had such a quiet yet firm authority, and was clearly so much in advance of them all. But one could see this trend at work in the minds of the first circle of male disciples. And in the long term, as one generation of Jeshua's followers succeeded the next, this process gathered momentum. It might have been offset by an energy and heart-based process along the lines of the Gnostic tradition, but sadly that tradition did not survive long enough to make lasting changes in the development of mainstream Christianity.

Comment by Stuart: The Gnostics were a loosely-knit movement which was active during the very earliest years of Christianity. They believed in a mystical state of Deep Knowing or *Gnosis* in which the knower and the known merge and become one.

The session continues:

Alariel: The boldest among the non-Essene male disciples went so far as to mutter amongst themselves that Jeshua had started to "feminize" the tough, heroic, patriarchal core of Judaism by taking such an extraordinary line in his teaching. Those amongst the disciples, like Judas, who had sympathy with the Zealot position saw the teaching as promoting a feminine weakness in the Judaic consciousness at a time when a resolute, heroic and bold stand against Roman occupation was needed. Bear in mind that the male disciples were brought up in a Jewish culture that still believed in "an eye for an eye and a tooth for a tooth". The leap from that position to turning the other cheek and even loving your enemy was simply too big a step for them.

Comment by Stuart: The Zealots were a group of extremist Jews who saw themselves as Warriors for God, and hoped to expel the

Romans from Israel by force.

The session continues:

Joanna: And were the first circles of disciples the first to form?
*Alariel: Yes, and these were the people who had the closest link
with Jeshua. They were the ones who had dedicated
themselves before coming into incarnation to play a very
active role in spreading the word of the teachings. They
would travel with him as he went around the villages during
his Ministry, and they watched as the Way developed. Other
people who were major players in this story had chosen
other work. In the case of the second circle of male disciples
you have, for example, Joseph of Arimathea, a very major
player, but having so many other duties that it was not
possible for him to be a first circle disciple.*

Comment by Stuart: The term "the Way" is used here to describe
the spiritual path established by Jeshua, a path found in its purest
form in the Gnostic movement.

The session continues:

Joanna: There seems to be quite a contrast between the closely
related female disciples and the male disciples.
*Alariel: Yes. The male disciples were drawn from several areas
of Israel, and some were Essenes and some were not. This
was deliberate so that no one could dismiss the teaching as
a Galilean movement or an Essene cult.*
*The female disciples were bound to have a more
difficult task than the male disciples because they were
coming into a society that was so rigid and patriarchal. To
survive that and still be able to work and teach – how
difficult that was going to be. Even males who believed
generally in the teachings of Jeshua might not accept a*

woman in a teaching role.

The male disciples were independently-minded individuals and you could not say they were a close-knit team. There was no single universally-accepted leader among them. There was a conventional faction, led by Peter, and a progressive faction including Thomas, James and Philip. And then there was John somewhere in the middle trying the keep the peace, trying to pull everything together so they could function as a group.

Compare that with the very different group of female disciples. This was a very close-knit group, a group which had been working towards this moment over the centuries. Over many lives they had been gaining experience at various spiritual levels. They had been meeting at various Mystery Schools, they had been coming together and planning what they would do. So this group had been working on this project for a very long period of time, which was why they chose to assemble in a very close-knit extended family group, many of them being born about the same time. Their families were very interknit and closely connected, so there was an instinctive trust and solidarity amongst the female disciples that simply wasn't there in the case of the male disciples. The women were all telepathically linked, and formed one complete telepathic unit.

In addition to this link, this closeness and mutual trust, they had the advantage of having one leader, and that was Mary Anna. When Mary spoke, they all listened. She was a matriarch figure, a very substantial person of quiet authority. So if a meeting needed pulling together, Mary did that. If difficult decisions had to be made, Mary focused the group on the issue and saw that this was done.

So it was a close-knit team with one undoubted leader, totally different to the first circle of male disciples. And indeed the closeness of the team – and they obviously were a team – did not please the male disciples, who were wary *and suspicious from the beginning. They just did not react well to a group of twelve women all moving with one intent – they found that quite eerie, quite frightening. They didn't understand it, and so that was another motivation for them to marginalize the women disciples, and another reason to write all this out of history.*

So the story of the female disciples is a big story, and its time has come. Various members of this close-knit team will be stepping forward quite soon to tell their part in this story.

Joanna: When you were speaking, I could almost see them queuing up to come and speak and tell their story.

Alariel: Yes, their time has come! Other groups are now working on this as we speak. It will all come forward quite soon and much has yet to be told in this story. It's not only the first circle of female disciples, but the second, and to some extent the third circle as well. Many of these pioneers of the Way are now ready to tell their story, and it is a remarkable and inspiring story. Many things will flow from the information on the female disciples as they come forward. It is time for a shift in human consciousness. And the empowerment and leadership role of women is an essential element in leaving the past behind and beginning to access the full potential and creativity available within the human race as a whole. If you ignore or belittle the skills and creativity of half your population, many of the problems of the Earth will remain unsolved and insoluble.

A great deal of information was suppressed and marginalized, but now, after all these years, its time has come to go out into the world. And that is good, for it is not wise to suppress information. Also, it strengthens the recognition that God is balanced: masculine and feminine. And that if we attempt to perceive God in a very narrow, masculine way – or even in a narrow feminine way – that only leads to imbalance, and no good ever comes from that. So all this is going in one direction now, the direction of balance.

The whole point about the balanced male and female system of discipleship, as set up by Jeshua, is that it reflected the central balance of Father-Mother God. Father-Mother God is completely balanced, completely integrated and completely whole. If you try to take either the Father or Mother element out of this equation, the result is a major imbalance in perception. Any system that honors the Father energy and neglects the energy of the Divine Mother will lack flexibility, sensitivity, compassion and wisdom. It will tend to become rigid and brittle and will fragment into a number of competing elements.

It is one of the great tragedies of Western culture that all knowledge of the female disciples of Jeshua has been lost, and it is now time to restore that knowledge.

Comment by Stuart: The existence (or non-existence) of female disciples continues to affect attitudes and decisions right up to the present day. For example, the debate about the question of women bishops in the worldwide Anglican Church has thrown up the argument that this is impossible "because there were no women disciples." Despite this conservative view, women priests have been ordained within the Anglican Communion in America for 30 years, and by 2006 there were 12 women bishops in that Episcopal Church. In June of that year, this movement for change culminated in the election of Katharine Schori, Bishop of Nevada, as the Presiding Bishop of the Episcopal Church in the United States.

The information in this chapter is some of the most important material we received from Alariel. The hidden history of the women disciples is a key element in Western culture which has been denied to us for too long.

10

An Angelic Conference

Joanna: I expect there was a lot of angelic preparation for the birth of those who wished to become disciples of Jeshua. Could you tell us something about this please?

Alariel: Yes. Several decades before the birth of Jeshua a Conference was held in the Interlife, the time-space between lives, presided over by Archangel Michael. This Conference was attended by human beings not in incarnation, and by a number of angels, especially angels who guide and assist those preparing to incarnate. These angels included the recording angels who keep records of karmic links and soul connections between beings. Human beings who were in incarnation at that time attended the Conference during sleepstate.

The object of this Conference was firstly to gather and focus those volunteers who wished to assist in the forthcoming life and work of Jeshua. These volunteers included many souls who had worked with Jeshua before in a number of lifetimes, and could be said to constitute the "soul family" focusing around him. All spiritual Teachers gather a soul group of friends, colleagues, followers and supporters, and these would often wish to incarnate whenever their Teacher happens to be on Earth. When souls have worked with a Teacher over a number of lives, there is a strong but subtle connection linking them to the Teacher, and also to each other. This connection gets stronger over

93

many such lives, and is the reason you instinctively know you can trust a person who happens to be within your soul family, even if you have only just met them. In reality, you have only just met them in this life, so these shared experiences, and a shared recognition of the essence of the Teacher, bind you together with links stronger than those of parent and child, or brother and sister. These are the people you have trusted with your life in other times and places, and that kind of experience leaves a deep imprint on the soul.

The second object of the Conference was to begin to plan how these souls might come together around the Teacher in a certain time and a certain place: that is Israel two thousand years ago. The angels started to investigate suitable families for the incoming souls, consulting the records of soul connections and karmic links, so that these souls would have reached adulthood at the time that Jeshua began his teaching work. They worked to orchestrate – we can think of no better word – all the subtle threads of these connections, together with possible parentage, so that the incoming souls would be born at the right time.

The overarching aim was the building of a strong team of disciples around Jeshua, especially those in the first and second circles of disciples, both male and female. The connections between the female disciples were given the greatest attention of all, for it was recognized that these disciples would have the hardest task.

As you have seen from the list of first circle female disciples, they were all related to Jeshua, either directly or through marriage. The older ones – Mary Anna, Helena Salome, Mary Jacoby, Martha of Bethany and her sister Mary – had time to form strong bonds of friendship and co-operation before the Ministry of Jeshua began. The younger ones grew up together and rediscovered age-old friendships from their earliest years. All these connections served to fuse the first circle of female disciples into a single,

94

dedicated and tightly-knit team whose fierce loyalty and intuitive linking enabled them to think, feel and act as one.

The male disciples, containing some relatives, but coming from different areas of Israel never achieved this degree of closeness and coordination, nor did they need to. Their task was to present a diverse spectrum so that the Way could never be dismissed as just a maverick branch of the greater Essene family. The power and commitment of the male disciples within the first circle was such that they would have been taken seriously, even if they stood alone.

The female disciples, working within the inflexible and patriarchal Judaic society of that time, were never in such a fortunate position. If they could not stand together, they had little chance of influencing anyone and spreading the ideas and teachings of Jeshua. As isolated women in a rigid society, they would simply not have been taken seriously. So their close family connections, resulting from close soul connections developed through many lifetimes, were a necessary part of ensuring that they could do their work. Thus a potential weakness in this group was turned into a strength through the hard work of many angels in the setting up of this grouping, and the goodwill and outstanding heart quality of all within the group. If one was looking for a good demonstration of the Way that Jeshua taught, one might cite the harmonious collaboration within this group of women. And this is all the more remarkable when set against the rivalry, tension and suspicion that characterized relationships between some members of the male group.

Comment by Stuart: We found the account of this Conference fascinating. Here you can see the early planning pulling the threads together so that the team around Jeshua, male and female, would be in place for the vital time of his Ministry. As the Essenes worked to support and protect Jeshua on the plane of physical reality, there was another team at work on the angelic level to ensure the success of the whole operation.

Comment by Joanna: This account by Alariel reminded me of an experience I had earlier in this life. During meditation I had remembered having a gathering in the Interlife before coming into this life. All my friends and relatives had gathered round, and it was as if we were choosing parts for a play. We were all deciding which roles we would play in each other's lives, volunteering to be brother, friend, workmate and so on. We were even trying out the different parts as if doing a rehearsal for a play. We also discussed when and where we would meet up in this next life, a fairly loose arrangement with a certain amount of flexibility. By now most of these characters have appeared in my life, but there are still some more to come! Stuart and I are still gathering old members of the Essene family together, and I expect this will continue.

Sometimes meeting someone from the soul family can be very emotional with a lot of heart energy – like meeting a very close friend you haven't seen for a long time. But sometimes, only one of you remembers.

11

The Two Marys

Joanna: Please tell us about the contrast between Mary Anna and Mary Magdalene.

Alariel: That contrast was very marked. They were both experienced initiates and empowered women, but their characters were very different.

Mary Anna was a person of quiet and calm authority. There was a great sense of clarity about her, and her dedication to the Light shone forth in everything she did. She acted as the spiritual anchor and foundation for the group of first circle female disciples, being well qualified to do so as she had been a high Initiate since the days of Akhenaten in Egypt. She was one of the brightest jewels in the main Egyptian Mystery School of that time, and achieved a balance and spiritual empowerment that made her the ideal leader for the first circle of female disciples.

Some people mistook the quietness of Mary's manner for docility or weakness, but when they looked into her eyes, they saw a quality of steely and unmovable determination that surprised them. A few might be foolish enough to start arguing with Mary Anna, but that look of determination made them change their minds very quickly. When you look into the eyes of a being that steady, that integrated and that dedicated, you know all argument is useless.

When she led the meetings of female disciples, Mary Anna would start off the discussion, but from that point on would say very little. She let everyone have their say and express themselves fully, and only when a matter had been thoroughly discussed, would she round this off with a balanced and moderate summary which acted as a fair consensus for the whole group.

Comment by Stuart: The impression one gets from reading the biblical account is that Mother Mary was overtaken by events that she neither expected nor could fully understand. And there is also the sense of Mary arriving at that point confused and somewhat unprepared. However, this information from Alariel gives a very different picture. Here Mary is seen working towards this vital time through the attainment of high levels of consciousness within the main Egyptian Mystery School. As Akhenaten lived some 1300 years before Jeshua was born, and Mary was a high Initiate at that time, we begin to glimpse a Master-soul of great inner strength and enduring dedication to the Light. And it was Light – symbolized by the Sun's disc – that formed a central focus of Akhenaten's vision of the Universe.

The session continues:

Alariel: Mary Magdalene had a very different temperament. Powerful, eager, enthusiastic, the fire of her total commitment to the Light burned within her like a bright flame. She was a passionate advocate for truth and justice, but in her zeal, might occasionally overstate the case, something that Mary Anna would never do. If Mary Anna's empowerment expressed itself in her poise and her restraint, Mary Magdalene's empowerment manifested in a confident and joyful outpouring of her energy and her love.

Peter, who had trouble dealing with any empowered woman and who had real difficulties with Helena Salome, had problems with Mary Magdalene from the very beginning. Her free and powerful expression of opinion, which might have seemed frank, open and engaging in a man, grated upon Peter's patriarchal nerves. Whilst he would never dare to question Mary Anna – one look from those eyes would have silenced him – questioning, and indeed criticizing Mary Magdalene was something that Peter did often.

Comment by Stuart: For some more information on Peter's difficulties with Helena Salome see *Bloodline of the Holy Grail* by Laurence Gardner, page 102.

The session continues:

Alariel: He deeply resented her closeness to Jeshua, and wished to promote the interests of the male disciples and diminish the importance of the women. He could not bear the thought that Jeshua could be telling Mary Magdalene things that he, the obvious leader (in his eyes at least) of the male disciples, needed to know. Above all, Peter could not accept the basic structure through which the Way would be spread: that after Jeshua left them the teachings would be given out in two ways. The outer teachings would be spread by most of the male disciples, led by Peter, who was to be the rock, *the foundation, of this new movement. Whilst the inner teachings (the Inner Mysteries of the Way) would be taught by John, James, Thomas and Philip, this group being led by Mary Magdalene.*

Mary, trained in the initiatory Mystery Schools of Egypt, was thoroughly familiar with this pattern of teaching because it was a method much used in Mystery Schools throughout the region. She saw the two teaching arms as mutually supportive because the outer group would be open and public and would deflect attention away from the inner, which in any case needed a quieter environment to do the subtle work along esoteric and Gnostic lines. In her view of things, the most advanced followers of the Way would naturally gravitate over time from the outer to the inner group, and this would give the whole movement a fluidity, a pattern of development, and a richness of potential experience that one level alone could never provide.

When, after the crucifixion James and Mary tried to explain this two-part plan to Peter, he brushed it off at once as impractical. He saw the followers of Jeshua as an embattled army, and regarded any kind of division as a splitting and weakening of their forces. Besides, Peter could not tolerate the idea of a rival leader, and a rival leader who happened to be a woman was quite unthinkable for him. He saw this move by James and Mary Magdalene as a attempt to weaken his leadership, and he simply would not tolerate it. In taking this position, Peter began the rift between the mainstream teaching of the Way (which in time became the Catholic and Orthodox Churches) and its Gnostic counterpart. This led to the final persecution and elimination of all Gnostics as heretics – a persecution which paradoxically was carried out by the very part of the movement – the outer Church, which had been designed to nourish and protect it.

Thus the clash of personalities between Peter and Mary Magdalene had profound implications for the development of Christianity, implications whose effects are felt right up to the present day. Although the outer aspect of the Way might develop (as it did) along religious lines and become a Church, the inner aspect was never truly a Church, but rather a spiritual movement of free kindred souls. A movement in which spirituality and not religion was the principal focus and driving force. As Islam has the Sufi movement and Judaism has the mystical Kabala, so Christianity should have had its own mystical and Gnostic core, and the loss of this core has left it with a permanent wound from which spiritually it has never recovered.

Joanna: Why didn't Jeshua make it clear that there would be this two-fold structure?

Alariel: Because he knew that Peter would have the greatest difficulty in accepting the key role of Mary Magdalene, and would probably have tried to isolate Mary and bar her from the inner group around Jeshua. Jeshua wished them to move towards the time of the crucifixion in as united a way as they could manage, and hoped that the shock of the traumatic events at that time would bring Peter to his senses so that he could accept a larger role for Mary Magdalene. Had this happened and had Peter and Mary gone forward united, the history of the West might have been very different, and the leadership role of women within Christianity might have been accepted from the beginning.

Joanna: And was Christianity very damaged by this split which started at the time of Mary and Peter?

Alariel: Yes, damaged so deeply that it could not fulfill its purpose as Jeshua had planned. Without its balancing Mystery School counterpart, the Church is like a clock with some of its mechanism missing. In a sense, you have not really experienced Christianity yet, only the incomplete fragment that history has handed down to you. Please don't go into judgment about this. That incomplete fragment has helped and inspired countless people since its foundation, but it could have been infinitely more effective as a way of treading the spiritual path that leads to the Light. A balanced system is always to be preferred to an imbalanced system, and only a balanced system can help human beings realize their full potential.

Comment by Stuart: When one realizes that the split between progressive and traditional elements was present from the very beginning of the Christian story, it makes the later pattern of development much easier to understand. What is interesting here is the way the clash of personalities – conventional, patriarchal Peter and outspoken, progressive Mary Magdalene – sets the wheels of history in motion in a certain direction. Sadly, the early pioneers of Christianity who came after Peter and Mary were unable to correct this initial divergence, and the split – which might only have been a temporary incident – became instead the general trend that resulted in the destruction of the Gnostic movement.

The session continues:

Joanna: Was the balance between the outer Church and the inner Mystery School practical and energetic or symbolic?

Alariel: It was both. The balance between the outer Church and the inner Mystery School was designed to provide a practical and effective system of spiritual development, but it was also a reflection of the essential nature of the Universe. The outer Church represents Father God, and also the Sun, Knowledge, Structure, Ritual and Form. The inner Mystery School represents Mother Goddess, and also the Moon, Wisdom, Flow, Process and Life. Neither is complete without the other, and together they manifest the wholeness of the Way.

The true Gnostics were not only Knowers of the Truth, they were Knowers of the Way. Within them, Knowledge and Wisdom, Structure and Flow, Ritual and Process merged into Oneness, as the masculine and feminine energies are blended into the ultimate Wholeness of Being. Here all the balancing energies merge into the totality of the human experience. This was what Christianity was designed to lead towards. This was the balanced path of spiritual development which Jeshua worked to establish upon the Earth, and this, sadly, was what was rejected in favor of a one-sided presentation that valued the Form, but rejected the Life.

Is it too late now to heal the rift,
to embrace both the Form and the Life
within a two-fold balanced system
of Church and Mystery School?
Will Masculine Structure
acknowledge the importance of Feminine Wisdom,
and will the Heir of Mary Magdalene
stand forth to balance the Heir of Peter?
We shall see.

12

Jeshua and Mary Magdalene

We had already explored the relationship of Jeshua and Mary Magdalene to some extent in *The Essenes, Children of the Light,* but we realized that Alariel might be able to take our understanding to a much deeper level. So we plucked up our courage and launched into the big question:

Joanna: There has been much speculation recently about whether Jeshua and Mary Magdalene had been married. Were they married?

Alariel: Jeshua and Mary Magdalene were spiritual partners. Yes, they did go through a marriage ceremony – the Wedding at Cana – but they were not man and wife in the conventional sense. They had important work to do together and marriage was simply the most effective way of achieving this within the rigid social customs of that time.

Several sources, including *The Holy Blood and the Holy Grail* (page 349), have pointed out that Jeshua would never have been consulted about the provision of wine at the Wedding in Cana if he had simply been a guest. However, if he had been the bridegroom, it would have been perfectly appropriate to bring this problem to him.

There has also been a good deal of speculation about the existence of a bloodline stretching from Jeshua and Mary Magdalene down to the present day, and involving the "Holy

Families of Britain" and the Merovingian Kings. All this depends upon the central question of whether Jeshua and Mary Magdalene had children.

The session continues:

Joanna : Did Jeshua and Mary Magdalene have any children?
Alariel: Ah, this is a key question. We will return to this at a later stage, but please try to keep an open mind on this for the time being.

Comment by Stuart: This answer was quite frustrating for us at the time because we sensed that Alariel knew a lot more than he was prepared to tell us here. But he had promised to "return to this," so we tried to be patient. For the moment, we went on with a more general question in the same area:

Joanna: Where did the wish to deny Jeshua and Mary were married come from?
Alariel: The tendency to deny that Jeshua was married, let alone married to a controversial figure like Mary Magdalene, came initially from deep within the Essene Brotherhood. In that era, it was accepted that a rabbi should be married, but Jeshua was not a mere rabbi, he was the Essene Teacher of Righteousness. The Essene priests, some of them almost obsessed with the concept of purity, insisted that their wonderful and long-awaited Teacher of Righteousness should be pristine and separate, above and beyond all earthly things.

The lay brothers on the other hand were much more open to the truth of the real relationship between Mary Magdalene and Jeshua. Knowing that even amongst their own ranks they were so deeply divided about this, the Essenes decided to keep the marriage of Jeshua and Mary secret, even to the non-Essene disciples. The Essenes were

104

very good at presenting a united front to the world and this they did most effectively. That attitude spread to other parts of Jewish society, so that it became taken for granted that Jeshua never married. It is only now, after all this time has passed, that the truth is coming out, and that the real role of Mary Magdalene – and the debt which the world owes her – is becoming publicly acknowledged.

Joanna: Was it essential for spiritual reasons that Jeshua and Mary Magdalene work closely together?

Alariel: Yes, completely essential. The energy required to initiate a big breakthrough needs to be balanced before it appears in full manifestation upon the Earth. Anchoring the Cosmic Energy of Love – Unconditional Love – upon Earth was a major project and needed powerful and balanced energy. No single human being could have accomplished that task. The crucifixion process was part of this, but just one part of it. Another part was the life which Jeshua and Mary shared, blending and aligning their energies and forming a single Star of Oneness, an energy vortex that created a portal through which this Love Energy could descend fully and anchor itself upon the Earth. This energy had long been available to the advanced few, but humanity as a whole could not access it before Jeshua and Mary anchored it through their balanced focus. Jeshua and Mary Magdalene worked upon this project together, they achieved this together and should be honored together.

Jeshua and Mary Magdalene, through their high intent and by invoking major angelic aid, were able to create a vortex of energy which functioned as a portal through which the Cosmic Energy of Love could descend into the vibrational conditions of the Earth and anchor securely within Earth-reality. If this energy had not been securely anchored on Earth, those who came after Jeshua would not have been able to lock onto it in their consciousness, and so could not have applied this energy in their lives. The vibration of Cosmic Love would then have been too subtle for their consciousness to sustain and hold. If that had happened, Jeshua would have become a mystical and legendary figure that no later generation could understand, and therefore no one could follow effectively. He would have passed into the world of myth and legend and his teachings would soon have been forgotten.

The great outpouring of this spiritual energy of Love affected the whole evolutionary process of human development. If you look at the arc of human history, there was a steady increase in the density of physical existence starting in Lemuria, accelerating during the Atlantean period and reaching a high point of physical density (and a corresponding low point of spiritual sensitivity) during the Roman Empire. The point at which Jeshua was born was the very nadir of spirituality on this planet, the lowest point of the devolutionary arc. Because Jeshua and Mary Magdalene moved human consciousness forward into an upward spiral, this opened up many new opportunities for human beings to rise in vibration and access higher levels of consciousness, subtler frequencies of Light and being, that would not have been possible within the previous downward spiral.

By turning the devolutionary spiral into an upward evolutionary one, Jeshua and Mary saved humanity from a long period of experience at a much lower level. Had this Love Energy not been anchored in Earth reality at that time, you would still be living now under the world-wide domination of a Roman Empire so depraved that you could scarcely begin to imagine the depths to which it would have sunk. Instead of turning round and moving up into Light from that time on, your planet would have plunged ever more deeply into darkness and despair.

The collaboration of Jeshua and Mary Magdalene saved humanity from all of that – and in this aspect of their work, the whole world has reason to be grateful to them.

106

Jeshua and Mary Magdalene saved humanity from the possibility of future sins, not the burden of past Karma. They saved you from all the sins that would have been committed if the darkness had continued to spread and the downward arc of devolution had not been turned into the upward arc of spiritual evolution. Jeshua and Mary Magdalene are the combined saviors of humanity, and should be honored as such.

We found this part of Alariel's testimony quite astounding, and it certainly sheds new light on the importance of Mary Magdalene. The idea of Jeshua and Mary as combined saviors is a very powerful one, and it shifts the focus from a Christian context into a new paradigm of spiritual development.

13

The Magdalene Legacy

During a session when Cathie Welchman was present, we focused on the status of Mary Magdalene within the Christian world.

Cathie: Why has the Church chosen to give such a bad press to Mary Magdalene?

Alariel: Mary Magdalene has been a profound problem for the Church over the centuries. In the early days of Christianity, it was not understood that the whole Universe is balanced from Father-Mother God downwards. Because this was not understood, the role of women as leaders and wisdom-bearers could not be understood, and a powerful woman seemed to be a threat to the whole patriarchal structure of the Church. So how do you deal with an empowered woman? You marginalize and malign her. You say she is a prostitute, and hope that no one will pay attention to her.

Joanna: So the Church was unable to understand Mary Magdalene's real importance and the significance of her work?

Alariel: Yes, quite unable. She worked with Jeshua to anchor the Energy of Unconditional Love into the vibrational fabric, the energy field, of the Earth. Their life together and the balancing of their energies as they worked side by side made this possible. This has been forgotten – or to be more exact, has never been understood. Mary Magdalene's part in this is not at all recognized.

Cathie: How did she do it? How did she anchor the energy?

Alariel: She anchored the energy by being the spiritual partner and close collaborator of Jeshua. And by putting up with all the negativity that came from the patriarchal Jews around her, while still remaining in that center of Unconditional Love.

Cathie: Was she criticized because she'd been married before?

Alariel: No, she hadn't been married before. She had been married on a sacred level in the Order of Isis: she had been married to Isis, to the essence of Truth and Wisdom, yes. And the fact that she was a Priestess of an Egyptian cult, something that would be regarded by the Pharisees as an alien and heathen cult, did her no good whatever in the eyes of conventional Jews.

Cathie: That's why they criticized her?

Alariel: Yes. In their eyes, it would have been better for her to have been a prostitute. A good, honest Jewish prostitute would have been looked upon with some distaste, but not the fear and loathing with which the Pharisees looked upon Mary Magdalene.

Cathie: Because they were frightened of her power?

Alariel: Yes. By going through the Isis initiations, she became a living Goddess. Are not patriarchal men always frightened of a Goddess? They had no weapons with which to fight a living Goddess. No valid weapons that they could use honestly in the light, so they only had the weapons of darkness to use against her, the lies and distortions.

Cathie: They also did something else interesting, and that is in the case of Jeshua they talked about "all his followers," but Mary Magdalene seemed to be completely on her own. Did she have no followers of her own as a Priestess of Isis?

Alariel: She had a great following amongst the female disciples of Jeshua. She was, if you like, the second in command in this group. If you take the first circle of female disciples, Mary Anna, the mother of Jeshua was definitely the leader. She had the most experience of this whole group, but Mary Magdalene was nearly upon her level. Mary Anna could have taken ascension back at the time of Akhenaten, when he presided over the main Mystery School in Egypt about 1300 years before Jeshua was born.

Cathie: So Mary Anna was also very much involved with Isis and the Egyptian system?

Alariel: Of course. Mary Anna was a very advanced being, but has not been given credit for this by the Church. She could have taken ascension long before, but she stayed to do this specific work. And Mary Magdalene was almost on Mary Anna's level, so there were two very advanced initiates heading up the group of female disciples.

Joanna: All this information on Mary Magdalene will come as a great surprise to many people.

Alariel: Yes, but it is an idea whose time has come. Let us be clear about what is involved here: that Jeshua had a partner of great spiritual attainment. And that Mary Magdalene achieved a level of understanding that went far beyond that of all the male disciples, with the sole exception of John. Consider what effect this might have upon the Churches. Will they be able to adapt to these new ideas, or will they retreat into a time-warp of self-imposed irrelevance? How can they turn the clock back when the time for change is upon them?

Out of all this one central question emerges:

> *How can any Christian organization*
> *deny leadership roles to women*
> *when one woman was the spiritual partner,*
> *closest collaborator,*
> *and chosen companion of its Founder?*

111

14

Some Key Questions

The first email we got from a reader when *The Essenes, Children of the Light* was published came from Gaynel Andrusko in Colorado. Gaynel's positive response and her enthusiasm came at a good time because we had no idea at that point how the book would be received. Gaynel emailed us with a long list of intelligent questions, and when we had the chance, we put a number of these to Alariel. We have also added some supplementary questions of our own.

Joanna: Would it have been possible for Jeshua's life to have taken a different direction so that he wasn't crucified but continued to teach the new Way so that this Way flourished?

Alariel: That is a very interesting question. Jeshua was responding to the consciousness of those he taught, and if that consciousness had been much more advanced he would not have needed to go through a crucifixion process. He could have taught in a much lighter fashion, and people could have reacted more positively.

However, human consciousness was very primitive at that time. The great mass of the people were very slow and limited in their consciousness, doggedly following customs and rituals, but having no great process of spiritual growth.

Joanna: Is the situation much better today? Do we have more people working at a higher level of consciousness?

Alariel: Oh yes. Very much greater numbers of people have

reached higher levels. The ability to connect with the higher self and with other people at very subtle levels is much better, and there are significant numbers of people who are quite advanced. Had there been that number of advanced people around at the time Jeshua lived in Israel, it would have made a big difference. This is also a time when a large number of people are waking up, and although the awakened souls are not in the majority yet, they are a substantial and vocal minority.

Joanna: Were Jeshua's teachings followed by many people who heard him speak?

Alariel: Sadly, no. Only a few were ready to change their lives. It requires courage to face the unknown and put aside the "little me" so that you can be reborn as the greater I – the I AM of the Spirit which unites all in Oneness.

The Way challenges its followers to become spiritual adults and move beyond fear into Love. Humanity was not ready to take that leap of courage two thousand years ago, which is why the Christian impulse developed along conventional religious lines.

Comment by Stuart: This is an interesting answer because it implies that a spiritual movement can only go forward at the speed which the majority of its followers can sustain. However advanced and enlightened Jeshua may have been, if most human beings at that point wanted – and needed – a reassuring and comforting religion rather than a challenging form of spirituality, then that is what would tend to emerge in the long run.

The session continues:

Joanna: Why were the Pharisees so frightened of Jeshua?

Alariel: Because there was a sense of power and mystery around him. He had the aura of a prophet, and conventional people are not comfortable with prophets. But also because his

114

teaching of Love and forgiveness leads to a transformative process that culminates in a deep Knowing of the Truth. When the Truth is really known, no priest or rabbi is required to interpret that Truth.

Joanna: Was the subsequent Church that evolved over the centuries very different from the intentions of Jeshua?

Alariel: Very different indeed. The Church developed gradually as the followers of Jeshua started to adapt the teachings so that they could more easily survive and flourish in the very hostile world of that time. The Way could so easily have been extinguished in the first two or three centuries of its existence. So decisions were made to make the Way more powerful, more able to survive, and more impressive to those who encountered it. All this was done with good intentions, but the result was to construct a complex hierarchy with rigid doctrines and elaborate and quasi-magical rituals. When faced with competing pagan religions focusing on magic, it was bound to be a great temptation for any new religion to increase its magical elements in order to survive and compete.

Joanna: Was the marginalizing of women part of the changes that were made in the early Church?

Alariel: Yes. The tendency to disempower and marginalize women had been present since the time of Peter, but it intensified as the Church structure developed and became more complex. The image of Jeshua's mother Mary as a humble, faithful and docile female was promoted, and the image of Mary Magdalene as an empowered woman and a pioneer of Christianity in her own right was attacked and denigrated. The implications for female Christians were obvious: the Church wanted women as compliant followers, not as empowered leaders.

After *The Essenes, Children of the Light* was published, one aspect of the unfolding story became the focus for frequent questions: If Jeshua did not die on the cross, and had managed to get safely out of Israel, what happened to him after that? We had been wondering for some time what Jeshua had done after the crucifixion, and were able to follow this up with Alariel.

Joanna: What did Jeshua do after the crucifixion?

Alariel: It was necessary for him to leave Israel. He could not have stayed because there were so many people who did not wish him well, and he could not have taught openly. He went secretly to Damascus, and from there along the old trade route eastwards. This route took him through cities which today would be called Baghdad, Teheran and Kabul, a long journey but eventually he reached India.

He had already studied in India before his Ministry began, partly with the Being that you know as Babaji. When he returned to India, he renewed his link with Babaji, who told him that the guru and disciple system in India, which by that time was already ancient, had started to fall into decay. Through greed and selfishness, many good aspirants were not being given the keys to empowerment, so that they stayed in a subservient role instead of rising in their turn to reach independent guru status.

Jeshua undertook to revive and refocus this system, which he did by traveling around India visiting the ashrams, teaching the gurus and re-establishing the original purity of the guru and disciple system. This work he did partly in collaboration with the disciple Thomas, who had reached India separately, and who linked up with him there. And in addition to this work, they also cleansed and strengthened the energies of a number of sacred sites. This was important as these sites were an integral part of the Hindu tradition.

Comment by Stuart: The Babaji referred to here is Haidakhan Babaji, who was described in *Autobiography of a Yogi* by Yogananda.

The session continues:

Joanna: On his way to Damascus did Jeshua spend some time on the island of Cyprus?

Alariel: Yes. Joseph of Arimathea had a big estate there, and it was the ideal place for Jeshua to rest and recover before the long journey eastwards. Joseph had made Cyprus the hub of his operations in the region, a wise decision considering the volatile situation in Israel. From Cyprus he could control the shipping of tin to all the Mediterranean ports where the Romans had a presence.

During a session with Cathie Welchman, we were able to follow up this area of enquiry with another question:

Cathie: Why didn't Jeshua return at some point to Europe if so many of his close relatives and followers, including Mary Magdalene, had gone to Britain and France?

Alariel: It was wiser for him not to go back. He knew that having given the teachings the Teacher has to step aside and let the pupils develop the work. The Teacher, having taught to a certain level, simply has to leave. This passes the full responsibility to the next generation, who are then free to grow and expand and explore in their own way.

Comment by Stuart: We commented on the events following the crucifixion in some detail in *The Essenes, Children of the Light.* We will round off this chapter with several questions we received from William Brune in Missouri. William emailed us after reading our first book, and we gathered his queries together in the form of a few key questions to put to Alariel. We have also added one or two follow-up questions of our own in order to cover the ground more thoroughly.

Joanna: What convinced the disciples to behave recklessly and preach openly when they knew it would be dangerous? Was it the resurrection? Or Jeshua's teachings? Or something else?

Alariel: It was partly Jeshua's teachings, but the "something else" was the descent of the Spirit. It was the breakthrough that many of the disciples made in their connection with the Spirit at that time which motivated them to preach openly. In the energy of the Spirit, anything is possible. This energy was intense at that time because so many disciples were stepping up and becoming teachers in their own right. So although it was a chaotic and traumatic time, it was also an exhilarating time because the Spirit was so much present.

Joanna: Did the impact of Jeshua's message depend on the fact that he defeated death as he had promised? In other words, was his message proved to be true by the resurrection?

Alariel: That is certainly an interesting question.

Truth does not depend upon events for proof and indeed proof in that sense simply does not exist. An Indian Yogi might outline an absurd proposition to you, and say he would prove it to be true by entering a death-like state, being buried in the ground and then being dug up some days later and revived. If this happens, and you witness it, does that prove the absurd proposition to be true? Of course not, it only proves that the Yogi has mastered the technique of entering a death-like state and then being revived.

Jeshua spoke Truth, and when someone speaks Truth, you know it in your heart. You feel the energy of the Spirit and it does not require a miraculous event to show you that what has been spoken is true.

However, the linking of Jeshua's message to the resurrection was perfectly understandable given the cultural climate of his day. Most religions at that time contained elements which today would be considered magical, *and it was then widely accepted that teachings would be authenticated by the miraculous events which surrounded the teacher. Given that climate of opinion, it was quite natural that the early Christians would seize upon the idea of the resurrection as a magical proof of Jeshua's teachings. Today you can see that Truth and events are two quite separate things, and in no way logically connected so that one proves the other. But this simply was not clear to people living two thousand years ago.*

Joanna: But resurrection is so much a part of the Church's teachings, for example, John 11.25: "I am the resurrection and the life."

Alariel: It is important to understand that the Bible was divinely inspired, but humanly edited. The original manuscript read: "I am the ascension and the life," but an editing scribe thought the word ascension *was a mistake and substituted* resurrection *for it. The sentence which follows, culminating in the words: "will never die," makes it clear that ascension was meant here, as any physical body (even a resurrected one) must die eventually, whereas a Light Body – the body of ascension – is immortal.*

Resurrection only gives you access to continued existence in a physical body, whereas ascension gives you access to Eternal Life. Would you rather have an extended physical life-span or as the Essenes put it, "Eternal joy in life without end"?

Joanna: Did Jeshua appear to his disciples in any form after the crucifixion?

Alariel: After the crucifixion Jeshua had reached a level of development where bilocation – which he had practiced before – became significantly easier for him. From that point on he was able to keep in touch with his mother, with Mary Magdalene and with all the key disciples on a regular basis through bilocating and talking with them.

Joanna: And people didn't understand bilocation two thousand years ago?

Alariel: Correct. Only Initiates of the Mystery Schools fully understood this process.

Joanna: All this happened a very long time ago. I feel the big question is: Why do we need to know these things now?

Alariel: Because there are so many energies within the Western tradition that need resolving.

Joanna: How do we resolve them when almost every church has a stained-glass window of the crucifixion over the altar?

Alariel: Let me help you to picture a church of the future. You go in and it's entirely light, and above the altar there is a beautiful stained-glass window which shows Jeshua and Mary Magdalene, hand in hand. And shown symbolically in the sky above them is the higher resonance of this partnership which is Father-Mother God.

This is a very different image isn't it, so light and life-enhancing. No pain, no suffering, just the essential balance of the Universe.

Joanna: Yes, that's very different, but where is all this leading to? How can we use this knowledge now?

Alariel: This knowledge will enable you to put the past into perspective, and release the energies of that time so that you can go forward.

When you begin to let go of the past, you become more open to the guidance you need to move your present consciousness forward into the Light.

Part Four:

The Glastonbury Connection

Avalon, the modern Glastonbury,
was a major center of education
and culture in Joseph's day,
and its reputation as a fount
of wisdom and spiritual knowledge
extended throughout much of Europe.

Alariel in Chapter 15

15

The Precepts of Joseph of Arimathea

Joanna: We know that several Essenes started writing accounts of the life and teaching of Jeshua, and it seems that a few of these accounts may have developed into Gospels. So did Joseph of Arimathea ever write a Gospel?

Alariel: Joseph was much too busy during his time in Israel to write a Gospel. But when he moved to Britain and settled in Avalon (the modern Glastonbury), he did develop a list of key points or Precepts which he polished until they took this form:

1. *Recognize that we are the union of the Spirit of the Heavens and the Substance of the Earth.*
2. *Honor Father Spirit and Mother Substance equally in your life.*
3. *Bring Spirit and Substance together to create a pathway to the Light.*
4. *Love Father-Mother God with all your heart and soul.*

1. *All the beings that you encounter are your neighbors upon the Earth.*
2. *The rocks, the trees, the animals are as much your neighbors*

as the men, women and children of the human kingdom.
3. *Honor all the kingdoms of life, and learn from each of them.*
4. *Love your neighbor as much as yourself, and yourself as much as your neighbor.*

1. *Forgive all beings and situations that you encounter – and be sure to forgive yourself.*

Comment by Stuart: These Precepts resonate with the energy and down-to-earth practicality of Joseph, the man of action. Not for him long, scholarly Gospels – a simple set of Precepts was much to be preferred. Look at the crisp directness of the way the points begin: "Honor" (twice), "Love" (twice), "Recognize," "Bring" and "Forgive". And there is even a hint of Joseph's sense of humor in the very last point.

When he came to Britain, Joseph would have seen the power of the oral tradition followed by the Druids. Has he adapted that principle in these nine simple points that could be easily remembered? And were these points counted off on the fingers – a common oral tradition practice? They certainly seem to lend themselves to this, with four points on the fingers of the left hand, four on the right hand, and the last point on the thumb. Could the emphasis on the oral passing down of these Precepts be the reason why no written copy of them has ever been found?

These Precepts are deeply rooted in the Essene tradition of the Heavenly Father and the Earthly Mother, and yet they also faithfully reflect the teaching of Jeshua. Could they be seen as a bridge between these two systems of thought, a *missing link* reconnecting Christianity to its Essene roots?

We also wanted to ask Alariel about the standing of Glastonbury as a center of learning at that period of time.

Joanna: The Isle of Avalon, the area which we now call Glastonbury, could you tell us how it compared in prestige with other European centers of learning in the time of Joseph?

Alariel: The Druids, and Druid wisdom in general, were very widely respected in the West during that time. We would go so far as to say that for a highly cultured European of that era there were really three main choices available. You could go to Greece and sit at the feet of the great philosophers, you could go to England and learn from the Druids, or you could go to Egypt and enter a Mystery School there. These three locations offered the peak experiences in education and spiritual growth available in that period, but there were subtle differences. The Greeks were more academic and intellectual, the Druids more esoteric and mystical and the Egyptians more occult, more concerned with energies and the practical working out of esoteric ideas. Thus Avalon, Athens and Alexandria formed a triad of centers of educational excellence, education taken in the original sense of both intellectual and spiritual growth. Avalon, the modern Glastonbury, was a major centre of education and culture in Joseph's day, and its reputation as a fount of wisdom and spiritual knowledge extended throughout much of Europe.

Comment by Joanna: Of course the victors always rewrite history in their own way, and the Romans made sure that the Druids were portrayed as uneducated barbarians.

The session continues:

Joanna: Did Joseph of Arimathea ever visit his sister Mary in southern France?

Alariel: Certainly. She lived not far from one of the main trading routes along which Joseph's tin was dispatched. There were regular convoys carrying the tin, and the Romans provided an escort of soldiers to ensure safe passage across Gaul.

There were several routes, but most of the supplies of tin went from Marazion in Cornwall across the channel to Morlaix in Brittany, then overland through Gaul to Limoges and south to Marseilles, where the tin was loaded on Joseph's ships for final delivery to the appropriate Roman ports around the Mediterranean.

Joseph would come with some of these convoys and would spend time with his sister Mary Anna, and Mary Magdalene and other friends and relatives in southern Gaul. These times were precious to him, like much-needed holidays in a busy life, and he looked forward to these periods of comparative tranquility spent with the people he loved most.

16

Mary Magdalene in Glastonbury

Joseph of Arimathea's connections with Glastonbury are well attested, but another connection with this area had also emerged for us to investigate. In February 2006, we received a letter from Bernadette in Australia who mentioned the Priestesses of Avalon, saying that they "were very powerful indeed." That intrigued us, and we were able to follow this up in a session with Alariel.

Joanna: Please could you tell us about the Priestesses of Avalon?
Alariel: An interesting question. The Priestesses of Avalon actually predate the Druidic impulse, as they are essentially an offshoot of the Lemurian Mother-Energy and Mother-Wisdom. They were able to receive this tradition because the Lemurian wisdom was kept alive by the Melchizedek teachers and then taught by the Kaloo.

Comment by Stuart: Lemuria was the legendary ancient continent which was reputed to cover much of what is now the Pacific Ocean.

The session continues:

Alariel: Mary Magdalene, a high Initiate of the Isis Mystery School, came to Avalon and opened up higher levels of the Mysteries and a deeper interpretation of the Mother-Energy as it had developed within the Isis tradition in Egypt. This reconnection at a higher level gave the Mystery School guided by the Priestesses of Avalon a completely new infusion of life, and the subsequent teaching and initiation of many by the Order made bright the last stage of the Druidic impulse in Britain. Through Mary, they were able to reconnect and re-empower the Order so that the Priestesses became recognized as a fount of empowered wisdom capable of balancing the power and wisdom of the Druids. The balancing of masculine and feminine energies achieved in this way paralleled the balance achieved so many centuries earlier on Atlantis, and was widely recognized as being a remarkable achievement by the wise ones throughout the Celtic world at that time.

So great was Mary Magdalene's grasp of the fundamentals of the Isis tradition, and so deep and profound was the wisdom that flowed from it, that she was able to interpret the existing rituals and teachings of the Priestesses of Avalon from a higher and more esoteric standpoint. Up to the point of Mary's arrival at Avalon, the Priestesses had some keys to the Mysteries, but much of their own teaching was still veiled and hidden from them. Mary brought the inner essence of these teachings out into the light, and enabled the Priestesses to understand their own tradition in a much more profound way.

For someone to come and make sense of rituals which you have been practicing for generations, so that the deepest resonances and symbolism within these rituals suddenly becomes clear to you, is a very powerful and inspiring thing. And this was why the Priestesses of Avalon were able to accept Mary so quickly. Mary Magdalene revealed connections and resonances, and a profound symbology that had always been there in the rituals, but had not previously been recognized. It is not too much to say that Mary's interpretation came as a revelation to the Priestesses of Avalon, who thought they knew and understood their own rituals perfectly well. But when a Master-soul stands before you and gently explains the deeper wisdom, all one can do is acknowledge that wisdom and feel blessed to have encountered such a wise and clear-seeing teacher.

It was in the role of teacher that Mary Magdalene shone, and her ability to inspire those who were fortunate enough to hear her made her a legend in her own lifetime. She brought the fire of wisdom down from the most subtle levels of consciousness and used it to help and to heal. And those lucky enough to be her followers and disciples valued her above all other teachers that they encountered, for Mary had the ability through her words, her energy and her unique presence to communicate the nature and essence of the All.

If you consider Mary Magdalene's work outside of Israel, her reinvigoration of the Order of the Priestesses of Avalon could be considered as a major achievement. There are some parallels here with the work of Jeshua. As he was reforming the guru system in India, Mary Magdalene was at about the same time doing very similar work in Britain through the Priestesses of Avalon. They were both reforming and reinvigorating an existing tradition through the application of wisdom at a deeper and more profound level.

Although Mary returned to continue her work in what is now France, the time she spent teaching the teachers at Avalon had a profound and beneficent effect on the whole Druid civilization. While the Druids revered Iesu, the Coming Savior, that Savior was not walking among them after the crucifixion, whereas Mary, a high Initiate with a unique link with Jeshua and unique insight into his teachings, was available for a time at Avalon to teach, inspire and guide. The teachers she taught inspired a whole generation of initiates in Britain, and from many other parts of Europe, for the news of a new spiritual dispensation within the Order of the Priestesses of Avalon soon traveled to other Celtic countries and brought a host of visitors eager to drink from this new fount of wisdom. And in many ways,

Mary's work provided the last and most elevated high peak of the whole long and illustrious Druid tradition.

Comment by Stuart: This was fascinating, because we associate Mary Magdalene much more with southern France (especially the Languedoc region) than with Avalon, which became the modern Glastonbury. But it seems that she spent some time here in Britain after the crucifixion, returning to settle in Languedoc where a number of her relatives and friends had gathered.

Part Five:

The Da Vinci Phenomenon

It is possible to resist
invasion by armies,
but much more powerful
is an idea
whose time has come.

Victor Hugo

17

The Cathars

One of the most extraordinary developments in recent times has been the Da Vinci phenomenon – beginning with the books *The Holy Blood and the Holy Grail* and *The Da Vinci Code* and peaking in *The Da Vinci Code* movie and a plethora of television programs, DVDs, books and articles exploring this same territory. One major aspect of the Da Vinci phenomenon is the story of the Cathars, and the link between the Cathars and Mary Magdalene. The Cathars were a movement of independent Christians, inspired by Gnostic ideals, which flourished mainly in southern France and northern Italy between 1140 and 1244 CE.

We were starting to get the feeling that the Cathars were coming into focus for us, and as our work with Cathie Welchman continued, we came across lives with a Cathar resonance. During separate sessions, Cathie relived two lives in southern France when she had contact with the Cathars. In the second of these, she was a young girl who was tortured and killed by the mercenary soldiers employed by the Roman Catholics; she had been a Cathar sympathizer at that time, but not actually a Cathar. In the first of these lives, she was a monk called Pierre, and we join him as a young man traveling with his father Joseph, the Abbot of Citeaux

Abbey near Dijon. This large Abbey was founded in 1098 as a Benedictine monastery, but reached the peak of its influence in the 13th century as part of the Cistercian Order. In its heyday, it owned a number of properties throughout France, including land near Mirepoix, which lies south west of Carcassonne.

Pierre: We're going to meet the Cathars in a fortified town, and most of the inhabitants are living openly as Cathars. They feel a sense of comradeship with us because we're all French and we're both afraid of what the Roman Pope is doing. We can only think he means to take over France, he wants the power. In our monastery, we follow the Way, the Way of the Magdalene and the Chalice.

Joanna: Can you tell me about the Way of the Magdalene and the Chalice?

Pierre: The Chalice is of Love...to do to the others what you would expect to be done to yourself. To dip into the Chalice is to link with all other healers, to feel as they feel, to expect to receive what you give out. That's why we're allowed to be married, it's part of the love of a human being. The Roman Church doesn't allow their priests to be married, it's a form of control. They must give all of their life to the Church and not have anything else interfere.

Here in France, it's been that way for centuries for the monasteries, trying to dispense love to the people and teach the people how to be – we're peacemakers. People come to us to receive compassion and forgiveness. We help them to understand how they should forgive and live with their neighbors in peace.

Joanna: Do you know where this teaching comes from?

Pierre: It comes from the Lord. The Lord sent his emissaries out, we received the word and we've been keeping it. It's not the Pope. The Pope is telling us to subjugate anyone who doesn't do what he says is right. That's not a path of peace.

Joanna: So you find some similarities with the Cathars?

Pierre: They're different, but they're still working to live peaceably with each other. They do have some strange religious practices that we don't have. Many people take a vow towards the end of their lives, but some take it earlier and they remain celibate – we don't do that.

Joanna: And it's all tied in with the Magdalene?

Pierre: We are.

Joanna: But are the Cathars also? Do they have some link with the Magdalene?

Pierre: I'm not sure...It's we who remind ourselves how the Magdalene came.

Joanna: How did the Magdalene come?

Pierre: She traveled with her kith and kin...sailing by sea...to our shores (at this point there was a pause and a sharp intake of breath as if the subject was experiencing a deep emotion).

Joanna: What's making you so sad?

Pierre: That she brought goodness into our land and it's all being destroyed by this evil man, this Pope. You can feel it, it's tangible. He's blowing black clouds over a region that's been peaceful for many centuries. We've grown in love and suddenly it's all changing. We have a history that goes right back, and the Pope is even destroying our history. He's burning books for no good reason.

Joanna: Is there a story of where the Magdalene came from?

Pierre: Yes. She came from the Holy Land to spread the word of the Lord to us. We've written about it in books and they've been destroyed. And we're trying to hide the knowledge, and it feels as if it's all coming to an end and we won't be able to live this way of life. We've never met the Cathars before because we've never needed to, but now we're traveling because the Papal edicts have decreed this is what we do, we travel and report back what the Cathars are doing. We know underneath that we'd rather side with the Cathars, but we must report back. We must write what we find. If we don't, we'll be in trouble...It feels very dangerous, this path.

We're on nobody's side. We can't be on the Cathar's side even though we'd prefer it because we're doing work for the Pope. We don't want to be on the Pope's side because he feels so dangerous. He feels as if he's coming straight from the devil. But of course, he's paying for the monastery to exist. The coffers in Rome are filled up and if you don't do as asked by your master...you'll cease to exist. And we must protect the Way of the Magdalene somehow. The message of the Magdalene was to share bread with everyone you love, share. Remember, in love, to understand your neighbor. The best way to understand your neighbor is to break bread and eat with them, share. Many, many quarrels have been settled over a meal.

Joanna: And also the healing was very important?

Pierre: We're getting to the point now where we can't even give people healing. The Pope has set up apothecaries...and they give a potion which doesn't do anything for the people.

Comment by Stuart: That was the last significant thing to come from Cathies's life as Pierre. It had given us an interesting view of the Cathars from a sympathetic French standpoint, even if that view had come from within the Catholic Church. One interesting thing about Pierre's life is how it points up the sharp differences between the French Catholics and the Italian Catholics focusing through Rome. In the Italian view, Mother Mary was the all-important female icon, and Mary Magdalene might be accepted as a peripheral witness, but never as a major teacher and leader.

From this account, it seems clear that the Magdalene tradition in southern France had been kept alive for 1200 years, becoming absorbed within the twelfth century monastic culture of the Languedoc region. How widely this tradition was accepted by the monastic Orders in this region is not clear. Perhaps some local beliefs may have been tolerated for a time, but a succession of Italian Popes steadily increased the centralization of control over Catholic life.

Information on the Cathar period – once of interest only to historians – has now started to reach a much wider audience, largely due to *The Da Vinci Code*, and to *The Holy Blood and the Holy Grail*. This has opened up a number of questions, one of which was a legend which had intrigued us. This legend focuses on a fortified town in the Languedoc region of southern France called Montsegur, which was beseiged by Papal forces in 1244 CE. The Cathar stronghold stood on top of a small, steep-sided mountain, and when the beseiging forces took the fortress, they dragged down and killed over two hundred Cathars. It is said that a small band of Cathars, perhaps only three or four, had escaped by climbing down from Montsegur on the night before that fortress was captured. They were said to have carried away with them something of great value, and we were able to ask Alariel about this.

Joanna: When the small group of Cathars escaped from Montsegur, what did they carry away with them?

Alariel: Their most precious scroll dating from the time of the Gnostics, demonstrating that there was a direct link between the Gnostic tradition and the Cathars. This scroll was ancient by that time, and it was much revered by the Cathars.

Yet sadly, the Cathars had nowhere safe to go to. No one wished to be associated with them in case they should face the same fate. And after the massacres in southern France, it became very dangerous even to be seen talking with a Cathar, or giving them shelter.

Joanna: And how would you assess the Cathar movement as a whole?

Alariel: The Cathars provided in Languedoc an alternative focus of Christian culture, a focus which respected the Earth and honored the Sacred Feminine. However, it was not as pure a form of Christianity as the Gnostic movement, and some aspects of Cathar theology can only be described as eccentric. Yet for the most part, the Cathars did live in Unconditional Love and Christian Harmony at a time when this was almost unknown anywhere else in Europe.

Comment by Joanna: The Cathars in southern France were the descendants of those who followed Mary Magdalene's teachings, the Inner teachings – so they followed a course very much more as the Inner teachings were supposed to be. The Cathars' lifestyle and teaching was also very close to the Essene way.

The Catholic Church did not like the way the Cathars rejected Papal authority, and this led to the Crusade against them and the persecution and death of most of the Cathars. The Cathar teachings were also deliberately distorted so that the Catholics could justify destroying the whole Cathar movement.

18

Da Vinci Symbolism

We were intrigued by the symbolism which underlies the work of Leonardo da Vinci, and were able to ask Alariel about this.

Joanna: The painting of the *Last Supper* by da Vinci – the figure to the left of Jeshua – is this John or Mary Magdalene?

Alariel: If you tune in to the energy of the figures in this painting, it's very clear that this figure is not projecting masculine energy. It's not a young man, this is Mary Magdalene.

Da Vinci had a very nimble and subtle consciousness, although he very rarely talked about his beliefs. He held many possibilities within his mind, one of which was that he might, in a previous life, have been the disciple John. Because he had focused on this possibility, the painting held a powerful significance for him. By associating himself with John, in effect he was saying, "I can't be there in the picture because I'm the painter. But Mary Magdalene can take my place – after all, we are both beloved disciples!"

When he was painting this picture, Leonardo was attuning to the events around the Last Supper, and it is the depth of that experience which communicates itself to those who see the painting. Although the layout had to be adapted to fit the available space, there is still a fundamental truth about the painting which strikes a powerful chord in the observer.

Look at the basic design: between Mary and Jeshua there is a central focus of energy, on one side the feminine energy and on the other the masculine energy – it is perfectly balanced. The two figures are balanced and they're both leaning away at the same angle. Neither dominates and the masculine and feminine balance each other in the painting as Jeshua and Mary Magdalene balanced each other in life. So there was much symbolism here and it was entirely intentional that this was so.

Joanna: I understand that as he was getting patronage from the Church at that time he couldn't very well put in several females.

Alariel: No, and he couldn't put in more than twelve disciples. But he managed it in a very clever way, he put in Mary instead of John and left the rest to the imagination. Rather a brilliant solution, isn't it?

Joanna: We've noticed that much of the controversial material about Mary Magdalene is being presented now in a fictional form. Would you like to comment on this please?

Alariel: When an idea is particularly challenging, your culture often needs to explore it first at the fictional level before moving on to absorb it as fact. At the level of fiction – perhaps even fantasy – your consciousness is able to accept these ideas without disturbing your belief system. Here you can mull over these ideas, and get used to them. When you find that they are not so dangerous as you might have thought, they are ready to shift over into the realm of fact and be widely accepted throughout your culture.

In this way your creative artists are helping you to broaden your belief-system and move your culture on. A general principle emerges from this:

What is seen as today's fantasy
may be accepted as tomorrow's fact.

19

The Existence of a Bloodline

One vital question about Mary Magdalene remained to be answered. We had asked it earlier – it was so important and so central that we were eager to investigate it – but Alariel had declined to answer at that point, and now we felt it was time to revisit it.

Joanna: You said you would return to the question of whether Jeshua and Mary Magdalene had children. Could we ask about this now? Did they have children?

Alariel: Yes – at least they had one child. Just after the crucifixion, Mary and her three-year-old daughter left Israel on board one of Joseph of Arimathea's ships. Her party landed in southern France, then known as Gaul, and she had much help and support there from the Jewish community.

Joanna: Did Mary Magdalene have any close relatives waiting for her in France?

Alariel: Yes. Isaac the brother of Mary Anna had moved to the Languedoc region with his wife Tabitha. They were joined by their daughter, the disciple Sara, and her husband Philip. By that time, Isaac's brother Jacob had also moved to Languedoc, so there was a complete family network there to support Mary.

Joanna: Did having all these advanced people settled in one area affect the vibrational levels in Languedoc?

Alariel: Very much so. Such a gathering of advanced initiates, centered around Mary Magdalene who focused the energy of the Sacred Feminine, led to the development of an advanced and subtle spiritual culture in that area. The power of the Sacred Feminine increased in the hearts and minds of the people there, culminating in its expression in the Cathar impulse about 1200 years after the arrival of Mary Magdalene. And all this began with the arrival of Mary and her extended family group. There was already an established Jewish community in Languedoc when they arrived, so the way was smoothed for them.

Joanna: Was Mary Magdalene's child called Sarah?

Alariel: Yes and no. Sarah was more of a title than a name, a title acknowledging her special lineage. Her real name was Anna; she was named in honor of Jeshua's grandmother.

Comment by Stuart: There is a reference in Laurence Gardner's book *The Magdalene Legacy* (pages 31 and 32) which clarifies this. The author points out that where a name is a *distinction* (like Sarah, which means "princess") it should be hyphenated, and he gives the example of Sarah-Salome. Mary Magdalene's daughter should therefore be called "Sarah-Anna" and we have followed this practice in referring to her.

The session continues:

Joanna: Something has been puzzling me. If Jeshua and Mary married during his Ministry, how could their daughter have been three years old at the time of the crucifixion?

Alariel: The scribes who put the Gospels together focused very much on the period of the three-year Ministry, and sometimes adapted the chronology a little to suit this approach. The Wedding at Cana actually took place five years before the crucifixion.

Joanna: And did a bloodline extend from Sarah-Anna?

Alariel: Yes, reaching down to the present day. Sarah-Anna is the Unknown Princess of the Western world, just as Mary Magdalene is the Unknown Queen. They were not concerned about being known, because their Kingdom was not of this world.

Joanna: In any case, Jeshua and Mary Magdalene wouldn't have had children in order to start a dynasty, would they?

Alariel: Absolutely not! They were working for the Kingdom of Heaven and had no interest in planting descendants on the throne of Israel, or any other throne. To determine whether Jeshua was concerned with the kingdoms of this world, just examine his focus. The Gospels are not political tracts designed to promote the overthrow of Roman authority and the setting up of a Jewish dynasty, but spiritual documents focused on the Light. Even when Jeshua was asked whether Jews should pay the Roman taxes, he still managed to turn this into an affirmation of the primacy of God. This is not the answer of a Zealot rabble-rouser intent upon throwing out the Romans and putting his children upon some worldly throne.

Comment by Stuart: The biblical reference is to the Gospel of Luke, Chapter 20.

The session continues:

Joanna: If it was never intended that their descendants should form a dynasty, what was their real purpose?

Alariel: They were – and are – a continuing counterweight to the patriarchal energy that has come to dominate the Western world. The descendants of Mary Magdalene carry the energy of the Sacred Feminine, with all its potential for balance and healing. The Magdalene lineage has provided a suitable channel through which many of the Priestesses of Isis could incarnate, so that the Isis vibrational frequency could continue to serve and bless the Earth. From our point of view this is much more important and beneficial for humanity than any dynasty of kings.

Joanna: So there was just this one daughter?

Alariel: Yes, but the situation here is a little more complex than most people realize. Advanced Beings like Jeshua and Mary Magdalene have options that are not available to the average person: Sarah-Anna was Light Conceived, just as Jeshua had been Light Conceived. Light Conception is quite different from either the normal process of conception or from any cloning process. Through Light Conception, a child of either sex can be created and this process can provide suitable bodies for advanced souls who have evolved to very high levels.

Joanna: You appreciate there has been much speculation about a possible bloodline traced down from Mary Magdalene. Some writers name three children, two boys and a girl called Tamar.

Alariel: Yes, but this was a false trail, carefully constructed to divert attention away from the true bloodline. It was realized from the beginning that any child of Jeshua and Mary Magdalene might be at risk, so an elaborate plan was devised to protect the bloodline. During the period when Mary Magdalene lived in Languedoc, she lived with her daughter Sarah-Anna and with three children whose father had died. These children were cousins of Jeshua: the eldest was called Tamar Miriam and there were two boys, Jeshua and Josephes, also called Joses. Mary adopted them in Israel before the crucifixion, adoption being a common practice at that time of high adult mortality. These three children had, at the soul level, volunteered to provide a smokescreen, a shield for the true bloodline represented by Sarah-Anna.

It is a great privilege and a big spiritual opportunity to spend time in a family headed by an advanced Being such as

Mary Magdalene, and despite the risks involved, there was no shortage of volunteers at the soul level for this task. It was the descendants of these adopted children who eventually became the Merovingian Kings. As children of the House of David, they certainly had royal blood, but their bloodline was not quite as special as some people may have supposed.

Joanna: Much of the modern speculation about a bloodline focuses on whether there are now descendants of Jeshua and Mary still walking the Earth, and what might happen if they announced their presence here.

Alariel: It is important to look at the historical context. If these descendants stepped forward in a modern democracy, how would that democracy respond to them? Frankly, we question whether the heir of any ancient bloodline could assume a significant role in a modern democracy. It seems to us that your civilization has progressed too far along the line of individual empowerment for you to put the clock back and be ruled by a series of Priest-Kings in the style of ancient Egypt – that just wouldn't be relevant today. In comparison, the position of Mary Magdalene as the spiritual partner of Jeshua, and her role as an empowered and enlightened woman DOES have real relevance today, and this is what we suggest you focus on.

Comment by Stuart: This information opens doors onto a number of new possibilities, and enters subtle areas that we did not expect to be able to access. Although we had heard of Light Conception (it is mentioned in Chapter 10 of *Anna, Grandmother of Jesus* by Claire Heartsong) we had no idea of its technical basis. At this point, we were still quite confused about it, and we asked Alariel to explain the principles of Light Conception. His reply takes us into the next chapter.

20

Light Conception and DNA

Alariel: It is important to understand how a Light Conceived child is created: the mother provides the basic DNA, the father provides an imprint of consciousness at a subtle level, and the Spirit gives the ability to create new life. This involves activating a sequence of twelve DNA encodements which work together to initiate the process of conception. The Spirit also balances and integrates the DNA so that the child does not have any of the health problems that your scientists are now encountering with cloning. Because of this involvement by the Spirit, the health and constitution of a Light Conceived child will be stronger than that of most children.

In order to understand the father's part in Light Conception, it is necessary to look at DNA and explore its real nature. DNA exists on various levels, and some levels of the DNA carry keys to consciousness instead of acting as physical markers and indicators. There are interdimensional layers of DNA which stimulate openness, awareness and subtle abilities, like abstract thought. These higher layers of DNA open the door to aspects of consciousness, and establish connections so that these aspects can be explored and worked with. These levels of DNA hold the imprint of man as a cultural and spiritual being, as the lower levels hold his imprint as a physical being. The higher levels of DNA – including sequences that have not yet been decoded by your scientists – are the ones that carry the consciousness of the father during the process of Light Conception. You tend to see DNA as a basic transmitter of physical characteristics and tendencies, whereas it is really a comprehensive multidimensional information system. Your DNA not only indicates physical parameters, but also your total potential as an intellectual, cultural and spiritual being. The multidimensional levels of DNA sketch out your potential for awareness, sensitivity and subtle abilities of consciousness. You may not choose to develop the areas outlined in this way, but they are there for you in potential. In that sense, your DNA is a complete outline of potential – a blueprint of how far you can develop if you choose to do so.

Basically, the lower the level the DNA functions on, the greater will be the input from the parents. Physical DNA has a great deal of parental input in it, whereas the multidimensional DNA functioning at high levels reflects the qualities and expressions of the soul. The DNA as a whole lays down parameters for development – it's a kind of growth chart showing your potential at all levels.

Now that we have discussed the complexity of DNA, you are in a position to think clearly about Sarah-Anna and assess her real significance. Sarah-Anna is spiritually the child of Jeshua and Mary Magdalene, but genetically the child of Mary alone, as only one set of physical level DNA – the set which comes from the mother – is involved in Light Conception. Those who believe that there are descendents of Jeshua still alive on Earth carrying his DNA at the physical level have not understood the reality of this complex situation.

Although little is now known in the world about Light Conception, it was certainly known as a principle in the esoteric groups of Jeshua's day, and was spoken of in the Mystery Schools of that time. Nor was it as rare as some people have thought, for a number of people close to Jeshua were conceived in this way. Mary Anna, Mary Magdalene and John the Baptist were all Light Conceived. And if you consider the disciples of Jeshua, Sara the wife of Philip, and Mariam, the daughter of Rebekah were Light Conceived, too.

During a session with Cathie Welchman in October 2006, we had the opportunity to continue these investigations with Alariel. Cathie was trained as a biologist, and she was able to frame specific questions which helped us to explore Light Conception in greater detail.

Cathie: How does Light Conception occur at a DNA level?

Alariel: There must be two double strands of DNA for the process to work — that is clearly and widely understood. The question is, how do you produce two double strands if you're dealing genetically with only one double strand from the mother? So she has her double strand in place. Now, how does the rest of the DNA assemble? Well, the Spirit has to do that. It has to produce another double strand of DNA which curls around the mother's strand of DNA to create the child.

Cathie: On a physical level?

Alariel: Yes, ultimately on the physical level, but it goes down through all the levels until it can reach the physical. There are many frequencies of being from the Spirit down to the physical level, and through focusing on each frequency in turn, the Spirit cloaks itself further and further into materiality. Another way of expressing this is to say that the Light crystallizes or solidifies itself down until it manifests as the full substance of physical DNA. This is not Spirit creating DNA, but Spirit becoming DNA.

Cathie: So it keeps going down?

Alariel: The Light keeps going down until it reaches the physical level.

Cathie: So in effect it is like a physical mating of a male and female on the physical level?

Alariel: No physical male is involved, or to be more exact, he has contributed some higher level DNA, consciousness level DNA, but no physical DNA through a mating process.

Cathie: So when it gets down into a physical human, the Light has solidified and become physical male DNA?

Alariel: Exactly. The operation of the Spirit – working down through the levels – manifests at the final level in physical form. What is then produced is another double strand of DNA which matches up with the mother's strand. From that point on the sequence proceeds along conventional lines, but it has to reach that point. There are also minor adjustments to strengthen the DNA and see that no weakness that might have come from the mother's side causes the child unnecessary illnesses. So it is an enhanced DNA. It's not like a conventional mating process, the DNA is improved, it's enhanced. This produces a much stronger and better human being.

Cathie: So where does the physical masculine DNA have its starting point so that it can give physical characteristics to a baby? Otherwise, it would be a clone and would look exactly like the mother.

Alariel: The second strand of DNA has its starting point within the Spirit. Light goes down a series of steps until it finally becomes physical matter. This is a very subtle process, is it not?

Cathie: Yes, and what's the purpose of it?

Alariel: The purpose is to produce a much stronger and clearer consciousness embodied in a physical form. It's a much stronger body than the average, and it won't get ill so often because there are very few causes of possible illness within the DNA. It will still be a human body, but a much stronger than average one.

152

Cathie: But why is this done?

Alariel: If there is a very advanced soul who wishes to experience human life, that soul would be vibrating at too high a level to incarnate through a conventional mating process. Beings who resonate with desire are born through a desire-based process; beings who are beyond desire cannot be born in that way as the process itself would be incompatible with their consciousness. In order to come into incarnation, a being needs in its vibrational frequency to reflect the vibration of that being's consciousness. Hence advanced high-vibration beings can only incarnate in advanced high-vibration ways.

Cathie: So, is the spirit on the male side that is bringing down the physical DNA, the father as well as the child?

Alariel: The Spirit becomes the child, but where the father has a part in this is that he provides an imprint of consciousness through his spiritual partnership and collaboration with the mother. Through the process of living, not through one single act, but through the whole process of living together and sharing a spiritual partnership, he contributes high and subtle levels of DNA. But this is at the level of consciousness, not at the physical level.

Cathie: No, I don't mean that. I mean if you are a spirit, an advanced soul wanting to come to Earth, and you put your DNA down to mix with the woman, do you become the child as well as being the father?

Alariel: When we're talking about Spirit here, we're talking about THE Spirit with a capital 'S' not the spirit of an individual soul. The Spirit as a transpersonal Source of energy goes down through all the levels so that an incoming soul can incarnate because the DNA is complete right down to the physical level. It is not the incoming soul that does all this, it is not the father that does all this, it is the Spirit as a transpersonal energy that does all this. This is the element in Light Conception that people find most confusing; they are thinking in personal terms, whereas this process begins at the transpersonal level.

Cathie: So who is the real father of Jeshua?

Alariel: The real father of Jeshua is the Spirit, in the same way that the real father of Mary Magdalene is the Spirit, not an individual spirit but the transpersonal Spirit, the Divine energy.

Cathie: So that Spirit wasn't Jeshua making his own way down into matter?

Alariel: What is your question exactly about the birth of Jeshua?

Cathie: I'm trying to find out how Spirit makes it possible for Jeshua to be born by Light Conception – how this process is related to Jeshua himself.

Alariel: Ah, I see your question. Jeshua is related to Spirit which causes this Light Conception in the same way as you are related to Spirit. You are a Spark from the One Flame, let us call Spirit the "One Flame". You are a Spark of the One Flame as every human being is, as Jeshua is. When he is born, the One Flame, the transpersonal Spirit, facilitates this process, at the end of which a double strand of DNA is created, a strand that matches up with the double strand from the mother.

So that is the process, and in that sense any Light Conceived child is directly the Son or Daughter of God, whereas all other human beings are indirectly the Sons or Daughters of God. But even a Light Conceived child is not the Only Son or Only Daughter of God. All human beings share ultimately in this same state of being. We are touching here upon the misunderstanding in the original theology of the early Church Fathers which has caused so much confusion.

So it is the Spirit that manages and overlights the whole process. For the very most advanced and highest vibration soul, this is the only way they can get into a physical body.

Cathie: So in other words, the process isn't controlled by what we would call a spiritual being, an angel. It's simply a process?

Alariel: It's a process controlled by the Spirit. If you wish to interpret the Spirit as an angel, you can of course, but we don't see it that way. We see Spirit as an aspect of God.

Cathie: So how would Jeshua decide? What would he do? All right, he has been chosen to manifest on Earth and to be Light Conceived, what would he do to allow that to happen?

Alariel: Once it has been decided that Jeshua will manifest in this way, a team of angels facilitates this process, to make sure the timing is right, the mother is available at the right place and the right time. This is not something that happens in an arbitrary or random way. A team of angels will be involved in the planning of this process.

Cathie: Normally a soul would choose to go to a couple having had sex, man and wife together, but that process comes up with many diseases and genetic problems.

Alariel: Yes, there are many limitations. The whole point about Light Conception is to eliminate most of the limitations, so that the child is very much stronger.

Cathie: So why aren't all humans born by Light Conception?

Alariel: They haven't earned the right to be, not yet.

Cathie: What do they need to do to earn that right?

Alariel: They need to become very high vibrational beings, and most human beings have not done that yet. However, many of the New Children who are coming in from other star systems are already at that level, and they can only be born here through a Light Conception process. They could not arrive here in any other way.

Cathie: And there will be many of them?

Alariel: There will soon be many more Light Conceived children, so perhaps it's just as well that we have explored this today.

Cathie: How will you tell whether a person is Light Conceived?

Alariel: You will feel the energy, and in time you will get to know exactly how this energy feels. You'll get to feel it and you will recognize it.

Cathie: So coming back to the DNA, presumably the spirit of Jeshua, having been born as a human before, there would be certain characteristics that the angelic team wanted to put into physical form via this process of Light Conception, is that right?

Alariel: Jeshua had other incarnations before, but he had balanced his karma, so there were no limitations that he needed to put into the physical body.

Cathie: So, when he was coming down as a man born of a woman, how would certain male characteristics come in, like for example, whether he could have a beard or not, whether he had red hair or brown hair? How were these things chosen, or was it all at random?

Alariel: There was a process of choice in these characteristics, but this choice was exercised for Jeshua at the angelic level before all the main process of incarnation began.

Cathie: So how did the angels come to make these choices? Did they have a committee meeting?

Alariel: There was a meeting in which it was all decided. It would have been appropriate for example that he should have brown hair rather than blonde hair, given the region he was about to incarnate in. And it was appropriate that he would be fairly tall rather than very short.

Cathie: Well, he wouldn't have been so effective as a public speaker if he had been very short.

Alariel: Yes. Many choices were made simply because it was appropriate. This was generally agreed, and, if you like, the blueprint for the incarnation process was agreed at the angelic level. But the Spirit had to implement that blueprint, had to make sure that the blueprint was translated into the reality of the DNA, which became the reality of the child.

Cathie: What was Mary Magdalene's part in the process of Light Conception? What did she do to begin this whole process?

Alariel: It was Mary's focused intent, allied with the intent of Jeshua, that initiated the process. Their objective was to provide a pure lineage through which advanced beings could incarnate upon the Earth, a channel through which the initiates of Love and Light could manifest. To open a gateway for a series of Light Conceived beings, like a great chain of Light reaching into the future, is a noble venture and it received the immediate support and help of the angelic realm. Through intent, through prayer, and through invoking angelic aid, Jeshua and Mary Magdalene set in train the events which led to the creation of a Light Conceived child.

Cathie: Can we go into the twelve levels of encodement?

Alariel: There are twelve gateways in the DNA process, each gateway controlled by an encodement. Passing through a gateway gives access to the next stage in the process, and all twelve gateways have to be passed through before Light Conception can occur. It would be very difficult for us to explain exactly how these twelve gateways work, because you have no vocabulary in this area.

Joanna: Because it's a language of Light?

Alariel: Yes, and it's both subtle and vast. If you only knew how vast all this is, even how vast your own DNA is. You already know that it contains traces from your ancestral past, tendencies, limitations, tendencies towards weakness and disease, and so on. You know something of the history-carrying side of your DNA, and if you put that alongside the present functioning of your DNA within your lifetime, that is a beginning. But there is also the ability of DNA to be a blueprint for your future, to outline the development of consciousness on many levels. If you put all that together, then you begin to see how vast your DNA is.

Many of the higher levels of DNA are multidimensional, they're not physical at all, and they go way up, up into consciousness. They are there as a blueprint, a pattern of all your future development. They trace your rise into higher vibrational living, they trace your rise into ascension and beyond. You have a vast amount of learning and growing to do – that is why you have a vast amount of DNA!

Cathie: Absolutely.

Alariel: It's not "junk DNA" whatever they tell you. Everything is there for a purpose.

Cathie: Have we asked everything that Stuart needs to know to write about Light Conception?

Alariel: Yes, we have, and we're very grateful to you for teasing out the elements of this subject. Stuart could not have done this on his own, he doesn't have the training and background in biology that you have.

Joanna: But that's why we're working as a team.

Alariel: Indeed. All your jigsaw pieces fit together to make the greater picture.

Cathie: Thank you.

This had been an astounding session, with so much new information coming from it. The implications of this statement by Alariel are far reaching and profound. If the descendants of Mary Magdalene now living are genetically her descendants and NOT those of Jeshua (since the father contributes no physical level DNA to the process of Light Conception), then this puts the whole idea of a sacred bloodline into an entirely new context.

What we can see emerging here is a spiritual understanding which transcends the earlier more materialistic perception. Whilst some people might consider the genetic descendants of Jeshua to be ideal candidates as national sovereigns, a deeper understanding reveals a more advanced perspective that is not concerned with dynastic succession or temporal power.

Note: After we had completed this chapter, we started researching material on DNA, and the most advanced information we found was from Kryon at www.kryon.com/seminar.

21

The Power of the Magdalene

Joanna: What do you see as the real significance of Mary Magdalene and her relevance today?

Alariel: The real significance of the Magdalene is her role as an empowered and enlightened woman. She stands forth as a continuing inspiration to women all over the world.

Joanna: And our world has moved on a lot in the last two thousand years.

Alariel: Yes, and your world is now moving towards a state where each one of you is becoming your own sovereign, and your own priest or priestess. So where will that leave organizations which have provided these functions for you in the past?

In considering these things, the key question is where authority resides. The teachings of Jeshua put authority firmly within the transformative power of the Spirit. This is clearly reflected in one of the angelic summaries of his teachings:

> *The Spirit of God,*
> *working its miracle of change within the heart,*
> *becomes the ultimate authority,*
> *the agent of transformation,*
> *and the arbiter of Truth.*

Within the group around Jeshua, the clearest carrier of that Truth was Mary Magdalene.

Joanna: Surely it is a paradox that Mary Magdalene, the brightest and best disciple, and the human being closest to Jeshua, should become so feared and reviled by the Churches set up in his name. How could this ever have happened?

Alariel: It was precisely her effectiveness as a disciple – Jeshua called her, "The woman who understands the All" – that made her so dangerous. Even if she had NOT been the spiritual partner of Jeshua, her position as one of the most successful of his disciples would have been a continuing challenge to the authority of the patriarchal power-base within the emergent Church. The early Church Fathers were happy to accept Mary as the first "witness of the resurrection," but they wanted to confine her to a witness role and prevent her from becoming recognized as a teacher. All the other Apostles could teach, and become leaders of the emergent Church, but Mary was supposed to stay silent and just be a witness, an Apostle to the Apostles – but not to the world.

The early Church Fathers could not tolerate the idea of a woman who was a teacher in her own right. And they wished to move the Church in a direction which, over time, would consolidate patriarchal control. They had already started to develop Christianity from its beginnings as a God-centered presentation, steadily changing it until it became a Savior-centered presentation focusing on a Divine Savior-Hero. The concept of a Divine Hero was familiar to all those brought up in Hellenic or Roman culture, but quite alien to the Judaic tradition. The Jews perceived their long-awaited Messiah as a king of the Davidic line, a great prophet and the restorer of independence and glory to Israel, but NOT as the Son of God. Jewish tradition was quite different from Hellenic culture in this respect: a Greek

160

could aspire to become a god, but the Jews perceived God and humanity as being distinct and strictly separate.

The early Church Fathers were not held back by any constraints of this kind, and they were starting to blur the boundaries that separated the human Jeshua from the Divine Jesus. Within that context, Mary Magdalene was a major obstacle to Church ambitions. Mary's role as the spiritual partner of Jeshua drew attention to his humanity at a time when the Church leaders wanted to emphasize his Divinity as a way of increasing their power and authority. They reasoned that the more powerful the Founder of a religion was, the more power and respect his priests would be able to command.

The Church leaders viewed the growing veneration of Mary Magdalene as a direct threat to their power-base, and to the concept of a Divine Jesus that they wished to present. Rather than risk their presentation and their power being undermined, the early Church Fathers were prepared to revile Mary Magdalene, and falsely accuse her of being a prostitute.

The Church's treatment of Mary is not only a great paradox but one of the great injustices of the Western world. It is only now, after all these years, that this injustice is being exposed.

Joanna: It certainly seems that Mary Magdalene's ability to influence and inspire is increasing rather than diminishing.

Alariel: The Power of the Magdalene does not diminish or wither with the passing of time: she is the Wayshower, embodying the energy and wisdom of the Sacred Feminine and inspiring others to do the same. She held a unique position amongst the disciples of Jeshua and demonstrated in her life the transforming power of the Spirit. It was Mary Magdalene's ability to attune to the power of the Spirit that gave her the most complete understanding of the All. Whilst the disciples of Jeshua might be able to grasp the All intellectually, she absorbed the All into every level of her being and thus became the ideal living pattern of what discipleship should be.

Mary Magdalene and Jeshua demonstrated a new kind of partnership between two Advanced Beings. Their work on anchoring the energy of Love into the matrix of the Earth laid the foundations for all future expansion of the Light on this planet. And their partnership provides a new model to inspire human beings to reach up into higher frequencies of understanding and collaboration.

Through this new model, you begin to glimpse a better way forward, with man and woman working together in a greater harmony where each respects the different talents and abilities of the other. When you begin to absorb and act upon this principle, it will inevitably lead to a rethinking of the whole basis of relationships. So the partnership of Jeshua and Mary Magdalene was both real in itself and yet also deeply symbolic:

The partnership of Jeshua and Mary Magdalene reflects the ultimate balance of Father-Mother God which lies at the heart of the Universe.

This is why the image of Jeshua and Mary Magdalene, as partners going forward hand in hand, has such power to move hearts and minds. They embody a higher partnership between men and women, but they also point towards a fundamental truth about God and the Universe.

This is the message which the partnership of Jeshua and Mary Magdalene sends out into the world. This is the truth which your civilization has so long suppressed and denied. This is the reality which you are now challenged to acknowledge and accept.

Comment by Stuart: It was fascinating to watch Alariel unpick the strands that contribute to the power of Mary Magdalene. Here we begin to glimpse the real underlying significance and uniqueness of Mary, and this opens up many questions about her enduring influence.

Is this why she can still inspire and guide us, in a way that still has relevance in the modern world?

Is this the real secret of the Magdalene's power?

Is this why she speaks so clearly to us across the centuries, despite all the efforts to silence her?

Is the idea of Father-Mother God which she represents really so subversive and alien, or is it the fundamental nature of Reality?

And is this an idea whose time has come?

Part Six:

Past Life in Translation

Working with past lives continued,
including one session
in German,
thanks to a brilliant translator.

Chapter 1: The Story Begins

22

Channels of Light
and the Temple of Isis

In August 2006, we ventured into entirely new territory by experimenting with a past-life session in German.

Joanna writes: I had never done a multi-lingual past-life session up to that point, but I was game to have a try. It was not easy, but the session turned out well. Isabel Zaplana proved to be a tireless and very able translator, and her involvement was the vital factor which turned the session into a real success.

During this session, we focus on Michael Schaefer's sister, Dr. Ingrid Brechtel who lives in Weinheim, Germany. Ingrid replied to my questions in German, with a translation into English by Isabel. Having established a connection with a life at the time of Jeshua, this is how the session unfolded:

Ingrid: A picture of Jeshua...I am standing in front of it...and there are geometric shapes on it. The geometric shapes are connected with a ball of light. It is like an energy field which is forming around us with colors. There are crystals...behind Jeshua there are the crystals and there is information from the crystals that is going in to the communication.

Joanna: Is any of that information to be shared at this time?

(There was a pause and I sensed a feeling of sadness.)

Joanna: Do you have a sadness at the moment?
Ingrid: Yes. There is a tension which is blocking this information. I feel a tension in the throat...yes, yes. Now the tension is relaxing and now it's very light, white and bright. Everything is all right, it's fine.
Joanna: If there is some emotion to release then let it go because the story can then come through more clearly.
Ingrid: This information is coming back because we know what's going to happen. We know the major part was planned.
Joanna: Is there anything that you would like to say to Jeshua?
Ingrid: I hold this structure which you have given to me.
Joanna: Are you happy that you have this structure?
Ingrid: Yes.
Joanna: And it remains with you for all time?
Ingrid: Yes. (Gives a deep sigh.)
Joanna: Are there more things that you want to say to Jeshua?
Ingrid: There's a very strong connection with him. It's here very profoundly, this energy. It is being activated now.

At this point, we all felt the presence of a huge energy in the room.

Joanna: Were other people given this information?
Ingrid: No. People received this energy, but it was not activated then.
Joanna: And you are one of the people who can help to activate this in others?
Ingrid: Yes.
Joanna: Is this one of the jobs you have come in to do?
Ingrid: Yes, yes.
Joanna: Would you like to tell us anything about this?
Ingrid: Yes. I had to hold back during my training at the Temple of Isis where the activation of the crystals occurred. From

there it leads immediately to a point of Light which was very far away and there is another connection and it is very powerful. This connection, the crystal and the structure when it is activated, works on the blockage in the head and starts to release it. The dissolving of this blockage releases a great amount of energy. I can see it now...Now I can see Jeshua's face clearly. We were not able to say very much before.

Joanna: Did your training involve energetic exchanges and telepathy?

Ingrid: Yes.

Joanna: Is it difficult work to do?

Ingrid: Yes. There are only a few beings who could go through this training.

Joanna: What was the purpose of this training?

Ingrid: A strong connection to the center of the Earth to hold a Light channel open so that this channel could bring energy and information to the Earth.

Joanna: Was there a connection too with the people under the surface of the Earth?

Ingrid: Yes, there was a link between the people and the crystals. And all these crystals are beings and they are working with Light and Love.

Joanna: And this was bringing the Light into the Earth because the Earth had become very dark?

Ingrid: And this work might also have avoided the need for the crucifixion. The darkness was the cause of the blockage here (pointing to the third eye.)

Joanna: So this energy was needed to bring Light and Love to the planet, and also to support Jeshua and Mary?

Ingrid: Yes.

Joanna: Did it come to the people close to them and then spread out?

Ingrid: Yes.

Joanna: Jeshua and Mary held the central focus of the Light, but was the Light also fed to them so they could stay strong?
Ingrid: Exactly. Our group in the Temple of Isis was helping in this work. They were preparing for some time before.
Joanna: And then you taught the new young ones coming in?
Ingrid: Yes...We were not there physically at the crucifixion.
Joanna: So had you gone to another dimension?
Ingrid: Yes.
Joanna: Were you also working with the Priestesses in the Temple of Isis before you entered the other dimension?
Ingrid: We had this channel, this means of communication, which was clear and everything was put through it.

Comment by Stuart: This passage is interesting because what we're seeing here is a support structure for the process of working with the combined energy of Light and Love which was so central to the mission of Jeshua and Mary Magdalene. Although these two spiritual partners held the main focus for this operation, the Isis Sisterhood was clearly providing subtle power connections which made the whole project possible. Hence, although Jeshua and Mary Magdalene remain the undoubted leaders of this team, the highly trained and skilled work of others also made a significant contribution.

The session continues:

Joanna: Looking down from the other dimension, what do you feel was happening on the Earth at that time?
Ingrid: There were many Light channels that were built and held open, but there was very great stress and irritation on the planet and in the people.
Joanna: Before the crucifixion?
Ingrid: Yes. There were also beings who should not have been here and they were interfering.
Joanna: Beings from the heavens?

170

Ingrid: Yes, yes. When this energy is activated and fully dispersed throughout the Earth, these beings will not be able to interfere.

Joanna: From your perception looking down, what was the crucifixion of Jeshua all about?

Ingrid: Like opening a new channel of communication, with a strong violet color to it, and a channel to other dimensions, to other shapes, to other elements and materials, yes. But Jeshua didn't die on the cross.

Joanna: Because he had other work to do?

Ingrid: Yes.

Joanna: Was it more like a spiritual initiation for him?

Ingrid: Yes.

Joanna: So after the crucifixion, was your work over?

Ingrid : No.

Joanna: Did your work help to bring the energy of Love down to the planet?

Ingrid: Yes.

Joanna: And by seeing these geometric shapes, is this opening us to the new world that is to come?

Ingrid: These structures are already there, in the Earth but not physically present upon the Earth.

Joanna: Though everyone has been affected by them, can only a few people see them?

Ingrid: It's all ready for the new world.

Stuart: Geometrics triggering off new states of consciousness?

Ingrid: It's only the beginning. These new structures of the new consciousness are still very thin...a thin coating over the Earth. Through the channels of Light that are here, they are building up.

Joanna: As we help other people to increase their consciousness, does that strengthen these structures?

Ingrid: Yes. There are also channels from other universes that are bringing Light to strengthen these structures.

Joanna: So are the energy vortexes that come from the heavens working with the energies from the Earth?

Ingrid: Yes.

Joanna: Are some of these energy points interdimensional portals?

Ingrid: Yes. And they help more children, more beings, to come in to the Earth.

Stuart: And the new children will be able to work with these structures?

Ingrid: Yes. The new children will have a very different structure physically, a different geometry. The new children anchor the energy here.

Joanna: Is there anything else you would like to say about Jeshua and the crucifixion?

Ingrid: The crucifixion now feels completely different.

Joanna: And is this a message that we need to give out to the world?

Ingrid: Yes, yes. A moment. (There was a pause.) We saw Jeshua as a very physical person, but he didn't have much physical pain because he was Light, a Light Being.

Stuart: So can we see the crucifixion in a lighter way now?

Ingrid: Yes because the energy of God couldn't come through, the crucifixion was necessary to open the channels of Light. At the time of the crucifixion, the channels of fear and pain and sadness were dominant. There was this horizontal blockage so that the people could only see in a limited way.

Joanna: So at the time of the crucifixion the people were feeling pain and fear?

Ingrid: And the cross was a symbol for that. The horizontal line was a blockage for all the energy of Light and healing.

Stuart: And the crucifixion broke through this so that the Light could come down?

Ingrid: If we can bring this new concept to people and remove the image of Jeshua having pain on the cross, then we can release people from the fear and pain and sadness.

Joanna: How can we continue to work together?

Ingrid: The channel of Light they prepared even before Egypt and the Temple of Isis, and before the crucifixion, if we can feel it, if we tune into it, then it will be stored in our cells and we will carry this energy wherever we go.

Joanna: Would it go into the auric field?

Ingrid: Yes. Everybody has his or her specific geometry which connects with the Light. It's different from person to person. Jeshua often talked about the energies within us corresponding with the stars and the universes. When he spoke, his words made patterns of Light. When Jeshua taught, he focused points of Light and there was an energy field that formed around the people who listened to him. It is good to be conscious, to be aware of these Light channels, and work with the Light Beings on the Earth. There is a strong connection with the crystals and the dolphins. Through them, a new Light channel is being opened.

This had been a session with a remarkably clear and focused energy. We are most grateful to Ingrid for giving us the opportunity to explore these subtle areas of Light Work. It is not often that a past life session focuses on such high and subtle energy work, and this made it a particularly significant and memorable session for us.

Tuning in to the channel of Light seems a very positive thing to do, and the ability to store Light in our cells and "carry this energy wherever we go" is an inspiring concept.

173

Part Seven:

The New Children

Anthem of the New Children

We are the Builders of the Dawn,
the Seekers of the Light,
the Gentle Walkers of the Earth,
bringing the Coming Age to birth,
out of the fading night.

We are the Singers of the Stars,
the Dancers of the Day,
the Sowers of a Wiser Seed,
responding to this planet's need
to find a Better Way.

Stuart Wilson

23

The Bigger Picture

Alariel: To transcend your limitations and see the bigger picture, you need to have a balanced consciousness – one which has no major blocks or distortions. Any block or limitation diminishes one's ability to see the bigger picture. For example, thinking in terms of rigid categories like self-contained boxes takes you away from a holistic perception of things. You would only distort your thinking by imagining an entirely separate Essene Brotherhood, a separate Cathar movement and so on. These categories merge into one another in a dynamic way, so that there is a single continuum of life projected through the incarnation process over long periods of time. Thus, the same souls who experienced life in the Essene communities, moved on to become Gnostics, Cathars and Franciscans. Many of these are back in incarnation as Lightworkers, and some of them are now reappearing as the New Children. The New Children come from a variety of sources, and we'll explore those sources later on, but for the moment, just focus on the idea that some of these children will be coming from the Essene/Gnostic/Cathar/Franciscan stream of experience.

Comment by Stuart: This is a completely fresh way of looking at the New Children, those children with special gifts and talents who are now being born in increasing numbers. Seeing at least part of this group as the culmination of a whole cycle of evolutionary experience helps us to integrate the New Children into the broad sweep of spiritual evolution.

The session continues:

Alariel: Perceptions and values may change as you move through historical periods, but the focus of the soul remains the same. Human beings tend to reincarnate in soul groups: there is an Essene, a Buddhist, a Muslim and a Humanist soul group, amongst many other groupings. Often there is one central Teacher who inspires the entire soul group, and for the Essenes, this is Jeshua benJoseph.

Members of the soul group try (when in conference with their angelic advisors in the Interlife) to arrange to incarnate at the same time as their Teacher, or one of his leading pupils (like John, who became Francis of Assisi), so that not only can they learn from these spiritual Teachers, but they can also help and support them in their work. So in this way, each soul group becomes not only an intense community, projected through time, but also a dedicated and closely-integrated team. And the more you can visualize these soul groups moving through time, changing in presentation but retaining their essence, the more you can escape from the narrowness of rigid categories.

But thinking in terms of rigid categories is only one form of limitation. And even if you were entirely free from the more general cultural limitations which you share with your peer group, your consciousness could still be blocked and distorted in those areas where issues within the psyche remain to be resolved.

It is very difficult for a human being to see, acknowledge and understand a truth that relates to a wound in the psyche, some area of "unfinished business" where healing has yet to take place. When the healing does occur, insight into the truth linked to that area is restored, and you

178

are able to see things there with a new clarity.

Limitations in the psyche block perception of the truth, and the healing of those limitations restores insight and understanding to the consciousness. Hence, the more limitations you have removed from your psyche, the more clearly you can see things as they really are, enabling you to take in the bigger picture, the broad sweep of spiritual development and evolution.

Comment by Joanna: So many of the "old Essenes" have chosen in this life to incarnate into very difficult childhoods so that they can understand the kind of problems and blockages that many people experience. Many have become healers and work in one of the caring professions. These old souls have taken on these life-challenges for their soul growth.

24

The New Children

We were intrigued when Alariel told us that the work of his group was changing, and it became clear that the whole focus of the group was being realigned in a new direction.

Joanna: Could you tell us, please, about the new work which your group is now involved with?

Alariel: *The nature of our work is changing and our group is now giving much of its attention to the New Children. The whole of humanity is experiencing an arc of transformation which will move your consciousness forward at a rate that would have seemed impossible only a few years ago. Part of this arc of transformation is the seeding of the Earth with a new kind of human being, people who are much more flexible and open to change. These pioneers will be the exponents of a new consciousness upon the Earth, and their work will initiate a New Dawn in the spiritual evolution of humanity. These New Children are being born now, all over the world, in greater and greater numbers, and soon they will form a significant proportion of world population.*

Joanna: What name would you give collectively to all these new children? They have been called "Children of the New World" and "Children of the New Earth."

Alariel: *Yes, I like those names, but perhaps they are a little long for general use. That is why we simply call them "the New Children". First, we would like to provide a brief outline of these New Children to give you some kind of context.*

There are four main groups involved:

Indigo Children, born from about 1930 onwards, but first arriving in large numbers in the 1970s. Indigos are intelligent, aware, sensitive, powerful and vibrating at a higher rate than the average child. They have a broad range of creative, healing and consciousness-related powers and skills, which develop naturally as they grow older. They have no interest in any rigid system from the past and are adept at breaking through barriers and pioneering new ways of living. Because of this, they may often appear as maverick figures to their own peer-group.

Super-Psychic Children, born from about 1950 onwards although one or two appeared (like Uri Geller) a few years before this. The Super-Psychics possess a wide range of psychic and paranormal powers including telekinesis and the ability to "read" printed material using a hand or a foot instead of the eyes.

Super-Psychics are very challenging to anyone with a scientific training: they can transcend many of the established laws of physics, and they do this naturally and easily. They are here to expand what you believe is possible when dealing with physical matter.

Crystal Children, born from about 1980 onwards, with significant numbers coming in from 1990. Crystals are:
1.   Powerful, but super-sensitive and empathic.
2.   Highly intelligent, but often intuitive rather than academic.
3.   Accepting and inclusive rather than judgmental.
4.   Highly attuned to a whole range of subtle energies, including angelic energies. (This does not mean that Crystals are little angels all the time, especially when they are young!)

5.   *Focused on the Now and indifferent to any information which concentrates on the past.*
6.   *More inclined to share than to compete.*
7.   *Deeply into the practice of Oneness (or Unity Consciousness.)*

Rainbow Children, *born from about 2000 onwards. The Rainbows are the inheritors of the whole build-up of the new energies. These wise and gentle beings represent creativity beyond ego, life beyond separation and achievement beyond struggle. Performance at high and subtle levels of consciousness comes easily and naturally to the Rainbows, who simply flow through life in a way that other children may find awesome.*

The Super-Psychic Children are in quite a separate category from the other three groups. Indigos, Crystals and Rainbows form the main evolutionary stream, and are capable of transformation of consciousness in ways that the indigenous humanity (let us call them "Originals") finds difficult to understand. Indigo, Crystal and Rainbow Children get their names from the colors in the auric field that surrounds them.

Try to think of the New Children as a powerful and fluid wave of spiritual evolution, which can transcend the normal rigidities of consciousness that have so long been taken for granted. The wave is fluid in the sense that a child can be born as an Indigo and move on to become a Crystal, or be born as a Crystal and move on to become a Rainbow. As their consciousness expands and develops, it is natural for these children to move into subtler and more complex areas of consciousness, so that transition between stages comes easily to them.

The Super-Psychics belong to a different evolutionary stream, and do not so easily flow from one group to another within the threefold pattern of Indigo-Crystal-Rainbow. Most of these are advanced souls who have graduated from a series of Shamanic lives within the evolutionary stream of the Originals, although there are a small number coming in from similar cultures elsewhere in the galaxy. They are usually remarkably well-grounded and have a strong connection to the Earth. This is in contrast to the Indigo-Crystal-Rainbow wave which is much more star-linked as most of these children have come in (directly or indirectly) from a number of advanced star systems.

Comment by Joanna: We understand that even the "Originals" can move on to become Crystals and Rainbows, and there is some evidence for this in the auric photographs that have been taken over the last decade.

The session continues:

Joanna: The general consensus of opinion at present is that Indigos didn't come until the 1970s.

Alariel: If you go back to the 1930s, there were very few Indigos, let us call them "scouts". Their job was to test out the vibrational conditions on planet Earth and report back during sleepstate to the main body of souls who planned to come here as Indigos. Conditions were improving in the mid-1930s and for a time, it looked as if the main wave might be able to arrive around 1940. But then the world slid down into conflict and chaos during World War II, and the main wave was postponed. During that War, very few Indigos came, really only those who knew they had to reach a certain age-point by the 70s and 80s to do specific work. After the War, vibrational conditions were put back by the Cold War, so that the aftermath of World War II really lasted throughout the 1950s and 60s. Only by the 1970s, had the vibrational conditions begun to lift sufficiently to make the main wave of Indigos viable. They had been queuing up in the Interlife, we can assure you, and they were eager to

184

come, but conditions had to be right for them.

> *So there were a few early scouts to test out conditions, but in all cases, the main waves arrived later, and in the case of the Indigos, much later. Because of this "early scout" and "main wave" pattern, it is extremely difficult to assign dates to these waves simply by looking at possible arrivals in these categories as they start to incarnate. Only by looking at the souls descending into incarnation does the overall pattern and over-arching timescale start to become clear.*

Joanna: Why did these New Children start to come during the 1930s? What was so special about that time?

Alariel: From 1930 onwards, various codings started to fire in the energy matrix of the Earth. This was the beginning of a major awakening cycle for Gaia. From that point on, humanity – in parallel with Gaia – began decrystallizing out of form and into the flow of Spirit.

> *For the planet to go through this kind change, the breaking down of old conditions in consciousness is essential because Gaia and the consciousness of humanity are now linked into one continuum of energy. Because human consciousness and Gaia are linked, the energy of human awareness is a vital component in the transformation process. This means that Gaia can only travel forward vibrationally at the speed of the majority of human souls, but through this linkage, these souls are now presented with a unique opportunity to rise in consciousness in a way that would normally take many lives to accomplish.*

> *Because this situation is so important and is unique in your history, a unique system of help and support is being put in place to enable as many human beings as possible to take advantage of this opportunity. Your ancestors plodded wearily through many lifetimes to reach advanced levels of consciousness. You are being given the opportunity to do a*

similar transformation in just a few short years.

Part of this process of help and support is the closeness and accessibility of the angelic world, and another part is the arrival on your planet of the New Children.

Each of the four main groups contributes to the process of change in their own unique way:

> *The Indigos break down structure.*
> *The Super-Psychics break down rigidity in the scientific mind.*
> *The Crystals break down the illusion of separateness.*
> *The Rainbows build on these foundations by demonstrating Oneness, and creative and co-operative living.*

Taken together, the New Children form a complete system for breaking down rigidity, starting at the level of structure, moving through the mental and emotional levels and culminating with consciousness.

Comment by Joanna: I also believe there are Crystals with some Rainbow elements (and vice versa), so I don't think the categories are totally rigid.

The session continues:

Joanna: Surely there have always been exceptionally gifted children born on the Earth. Why are these New Children so different?

Alariel: Yes, there have been gifted and super-gifted children throughout your history, but please recognize that these children are of quite a different order. Because the gifted children in your past were the brightest and best of the stream of Originals, they were still bound by the limitations of human consciousness as a whole, and their skills, though remarkable, were essentially very highly developed human skills. The New Children are coming in from a variety of advanced star systems and have been used to exercising remarkable and subtle powers in their star system of origin. If a gifted child from the Original stream would be regarded with respect and admiration, some of these New Children will generate what we can only call awe. Their abilities are of a completely different order, and are not limited by Earth-culture or Earth-history. If we take the Crystals for example, why anyone should wish to study history just baffles them. The Crystal perspective can be summarized like this:

> *The study of history locks you*
> *into the paradigms of your ancestors:*
> *what you should be focusing on is the future,*
> *the paradigms of your children.*

What is also remarkable about the New Children is the extent to which they instinctively and intuitively share a common philosophy, and are determined to apply this philosophy in practical terms in their lives, come what may. When we talk of "philosophy," we do not mean a series of interconnected academic concepts, but rather a common theme and basis of belief. This theme is the Oneness of all life, a Oneness which may be explored intellectually and intuitively, but which is felt and recognized in the heart.

Though the commitment to Oneness is shared by all the New Children, it emerges as a key distinguishing feature of the Crystals, and underlies their focus on peace and non-violence. For the Crystals, separateness is an illusion, a lie, because they realize that Oneness is the deep reality of things. Crystals do not need to learn or study Oneness, they come into incarnation simply knowing it.

187

The Crystal Children are here to teach Love and how to transcend all the conflict and divisions of the past and go forward together in Oneness. Due to their commitment to Oneness, Crystals will be natural peace-makers and conciliators within their peer-group, and in the wider world when they reach maturity. This tendency to be inclusive can emerge at quite an early age, with Crystals reacting to any show of conflict or violence in quite original and creative ways. Even quite young Crystals, when subjected to any physical attack within their peer-group, might say something along the lines of, "I'm your friend. Why would you want to hit your friend?"

Ideally, the New Children will require special parenting and education specifically developed for their needs. They will probably be well ahead of their peers intellectually and creatively, and can feel isolated and rejected by the Originals in their peer-group. The New Children may still be emotionally immature and will have to go through all the usual emotional stages during their development, and they can throw tantrums with a capital T! Some will have problems with speech as they are accustomed to communicating telepathically on their planet of origin, and some may be dyslexic.

Although the New Children are essentially spiritual beings, do not imagine that they will be pious or docile – quite the opposite. They will be intelligent, imaginative, probing and questioning, and they may challenge all that you hold most dear. They have an uncanny ability to home in on hypocrisy and double standards, and may be outrageous in the way they expose human foibles and inconsistencies. All in all, parenting a New Child is going to be a more challenging – but more rewarding – process than parenting the average child.

The education of the New Child requires careful consideration. These children – especially the multi-talented and meta-gifted Crystal Children – will simply not put up with a rigid and limited educational framework. They will develop more rapidly than the average child, reading sooner and questioning deeper and quicker, and they need a supportive environment for this development.

Specialist education may not be feasible for many parents, and many New Children have elected to be taught in mainstream education, hard as that might be for them at times. They do have to mix with mainstream kids, and having a conventional education is one way that the New Children adjust to this need. While Indigos can at a pinch shine in conventional schooling, neither Crystals nor Rainbows will thrive in such a restrictive and over-controlling environment. Crystal Children in particular have specific educational needs that are difficult to address within any rigid teaching system. The two systems most suited to Crystal Children are Montessori and Steiner education. Of these, Montessori is the ideal because it is such a flexible system.

Comment by Stuart: Maria Montessori (1870-1952) and Rudolf Steiner (1861-1925) both set up systems of progressive, holistic and child-centered education.

Comment by Joanna: When I lived in the Western Australian bush, I worked in a kindergarten run on Montessori lines and much later in the UK trained to be a Montessori Pre-Primary and Primary teacher. I have worked in a Montessori school, and even had a Montessori school in my own home at one stage. All this background in Montessori education helps me to understand the special needs of the New Children, and makes me aware that a good Montessori school is an excellent way of educating these children. The Steiner/Waldorf system can also be recommended because it is so holistic, and I have first hand experience of this because two of my daughters attended a Steiner School for a while. For all parents who are involved with holistic education, I would also recommend rebirthing as a way of gaining insight into the birth experience and what it is like to be a child.

The session continues:

Joanna: Do Crystals sift through books in a new way, and do they have photographic memories?

Alariel: Photographic memory is a special skill, and a few of the New Children will have this, but it won't be universal amongst any of the sub-groups. What Crystals have is a more highly developed intuitive capacity, and that capacity enables them to scan through books quickly, accessing only what is significant and useful and leaving the rest. They have an instinct for what chapters and pages they should read, and what is unimportant and can be left. There are some Indigos with this Crystal ability to scan through books quickly, reading the significant and skipping the rest, but it's a very rare skill amongst Originals. It is not a kind of speed-reading, where every page is read, it is more an intuitive feeling into the organic structure and development of the book, leaving aside whole sections which are of no interest to the reader. It is a tuning in to how the text is developing (and how the mind of the writer is moving) in a very fluid, intuitive way, absorbing only information which is interesting and significant.

Joanna: There are some reports of Super-Psychic Children being able to read through their hands or feet. How does this work?

Alariel: They are turning the book's contents into energy and reading the energy. The hands or feet are just energy-sensors, but they're not acting like eyes looking at a page. When you get to the point that a book is printed it has an energetic field to it, and everything in that book is represented in the energy field. The author starts to build this field (even if quite unaware of it) as soon as he or she

190

starts working on planning a book. The more thought, emotion, and effort that are put into a book, the bigger and more powerful the field gets. That is why a major book project is almost impossible for an author to simply abandon and forget about; the energy field has become too strong.

As these children are reading the energy, rather than the words, this is why they can still read a page even when it has been crumpled up into a tiny ball. The Originals find it very difficult to understand this kind of ability, because it is so far beyond what they can accomplish.

Joanna: Yet many of these powers are there in potential for us, and we've just become lazy and haven't used any of what might be called our "sixth sense".

Alariel: Yes, that's true. In shamanic societies, this sort of skill would be better respected and understood. Many of these skills have been available to Originals for centuries, but they have just chosen not to develop them.

Joanna: Will the New Children demonstrate many special gifts?

Alariel: There are many different gifts, some starting to emerge through Indigos, but many more to come with the Crystal Children. Do not expect Crystals and Rainbows to have Super-Psychic gifts. Crystal Children are not interested in bending spoons, they're here to bend minds!

Joanna: So the three main groups feed one into the other?

Alariel: Yes. These groups are not rigid batches, but rather like flexible waves, with a few scouts starting off each wave and then much bigger numbers coming in at a later point when the conditions are known to be favorable.

Joanna: Do the Crystals have generally a more highly tuned sensitivity?

Alariel: Yes, broadly that is true. Crystals have a more highly tuned consciousness than Indigos, and it is the level of vibrational tuning which gives the clue to the existence of special abilities. Some Indigos are telepathic and empathic, but many Crystals will be. Indigos have had much more to "feel their way" here on this planet, as they were the first of these New Children to get here. That has made their approach more tentative, more cautious, and they spent longer in clarifying exactly what they could do here. Most Crystals come in just knowing why they are here, and that's why some Crystals will find schooling – any schooling – "a waste of time." They have arrived here bursting with information and skills and don't need too much training! However, they will still need to develop inter-personal skills, or they will find their audiences will not understand them and will not want to listen to them. They have to learn that having a lot to say is only the starting point. Then you have to learn how to communicate it effectively.

Joanna: Do the New Children prefer some locations to others?

Alariel: Generally speaking, they will avoid coming to parents living in cities, they just don't like the city vibration. They would prefer to come to parents living in rural areas, especially those where there is a strong "new age" or progressive element. However, they are also attracted to communities which have a spiritual focus, even if these communities follow some specific religion. Crystals and Rainbows especially are not interested in religion, but they are interested in spirituality, and the spiritual commitment of a community will attract them. They are really looking for flexible parents with open minds, who will respond to their special needs and their special gifts. And these parents can be found in many parts of the world. However, even these parents are unlikely to attract a Crystal or Rainbow child if they live in a war zone. Both these categories of New Child are committed to peace and Oneness and they will usually avoid a war zone or an occupied territory.

Joanna: Should we give these New Children special attention?

Alariel: Yes, because they come with a special mission, to break down the rigid patterns of the past and establish a new sense of Oneness. They come to heal the divisions of humanity, and

192

these divisions need to be healed quickly now. If you're going to benefit from a rapid spiritual evolution, you'll have to leave conflict behind. You have to learn to be inclusive rather than exclusive.

Joanna: One of our contacts has an Indigo child, and she says that she didn't give him any special attention. I'm not saying we should single them out for attention and say, "Hey, look, there's a special child." I'm saying that they just need to be handled in a different way to the Originals, and for parents to be aware of these differences.

Alariel: Yes, that's exactly right. Don't put them on pedestals as special beings, but try to give them appropriate handling, care and education. That will bring out their full potential. They have special gifts and their handling should be designed to help them exercise those gifts. These New Children don't want to be regarded as so special that they are separated from the Oneness. They believe in the Oneness and try to include everyone within that. Their position is that they see all human beings as having special gifts, special talents, and it's just that many have been asleep to the potential of the gifts that lie within them.

Joanna: Is it a danger that because of a lack of understanding or even derision, their talents may be suppressed and go underground?

Alariel: Yes, if their gifts are not understood they may be forced to conform to the world of their peer-group Originals. These New Children need to be recognized as having special gifts, but the specialness lies in the gifts, not in an ego-driven individuality. And that is a fine distinction that many Originals may find difficult to make.

Joanna: I see people that I recognize as Indigos going out in the world and spreading Light wherever they go, although they may not be conscious of doing that at all.

Alariel: Yes, all the New Children have this in common, that they are Bearers of Light. You can identify them more by what they do and the effects of what they do on other people, than by any description or labeling.

Joanna: Are some of the New Children taking drugs as a way of hiding behind them?

Alariel: That can happen, but not with the Super-Psychics so much because they are instinctively aware that, by taking drugs, they would get into areas where the psyche falls apart very quickly. Some individuals in the other groups, Indigos, Crystals and Rainbows may find they are so overwhelmed by the combination of their super-sensitivity and the dysfunctionality of the Originals around them, that they may take refuge in drugs for a while. The interesting thing about Crystals is that their recovery from any period of addiction will be remarkably rapid. They may hide in addiction, keeping their heads down so they don't attract attention, but when they wish to recover and get back on track, they will do so with ease and with great speed. The consciousness of Crystals is so attuned to wholeness that it is very difficult to fragment, and that is the key to understanding their remarkable ability to heal themselves.

Joanna: And some of the New Children may seem to have phobic tendencies?

Alariel: Yes, they may reflect the phobias of all the members of their family, and play out these phobias in dramatic ways, like an actor putting on a role. And this may be challenging for Originals who are not used to having their phobias mirrored back to them.

Joanna: And some may be dyslexic?

Alariel: Yes, it's an opportunity for them to get beyond linear thought and into more holistic forms of expression.

Joanna: How would you sum up the New Children in just a few words?

Alariel: The words would be sensitive, gifted and wise.

Joanna: I have the feeling that we're only just beginning to understand these New Children.

Alariel: You are in the very earliest stages of understanding the New Children, and all the gifts they bring to this planet. Think of it as beginning a voyage of discovery as you explore the nature and abilities of these wonderful children. And it is important to try to understand them because if you can do that, you can see where the consciousness of humanity is now headed. People who can't understand the New Children and remain rooted in paradigms of the past are trying to judge the future by past criteria and that just doesn't work. The only thing that anyone can say with certainty about your future is that it will be nothing like your past!

25

Crystal Children

Joanna: You mentioned the starry origins of the New Children. Where do the Crystals, for example, come from?

Alariel: Crystal Children are coming in from several galaxies to assist humanity at this time. They come from Sirius, Arcturus, the Pleiades, Orion and Andromeda, and from some star systems which are beyond the present means of your investigation, as they are located in a distant galaxy. But there are also Crystal Children who have had lives as, for example, Essenes and Cathars, and are returning now in a more advanced and sensitive form. They may at one time have been "Originals" as we term them, but they have now evolved and moved on to become Indigos or Crystal Children.

Joanna: Will Crystals show all the usual range of emotions in the process of growing up?

Alariel: Yes, and they will not be little angels all the time when they are young. They do have some brakes on their reactions: they will not, for instance, be violent even if those in their peer-group are habitually violent. Basically, Crystals come from a culture of total Oneness where violence is not in their vocabulary.

Joanna: Why are Crystals arriving in such large numbers now?

Alariel: To be teachers of the theory and practice of Oneness. They come to teach humanity that separation is a lie and that Oneness is the truth of life. The Earth cannot move forward in vibration with a humanity which is so deeply divided against itself. All this tension and conflict needs sweeping away. The Crystals are masters of reconciliation, but they need help and support if they are to have a big impact on human consciousness as a whole.

Joanna: The Crystals seem to be building on the new foundations that are available now, since the Indigos have broken down so many old structures.

Alariel: Breaking down those structures has opened many minds to new frequencies of consciousness and a new way of living based on co-operation rather than conflict.

Joanna: I see examples of these changes everywhere. For example, many primary schools are now using sensitivity exercises.

Alariel: Yes, this shows you the direction of your culture as a whole, becoming much more aware that levels of sensitivity do exist, and seeing sensitivity as a benefit rather than a burden. This works very well for the Originals, but some Crystals may be too sensitive already, and may need their sensitivity shut down gently because it is too painful for them to relate to the Originals in their class at school. That is a skill which needs to be developed and would be useful for parents of Crystal Children. You don't always want to increase the sensitivity of Crystals, that might only increase their pain in dealing with their peer-group.

Joanna: What is the most difficult time for Crystals?

Alariel: The primary school stage. Unless their parents can find some way of partially damping down their sensitivity from time to time, it may be a rough ride for many Crystals through the average primary school system. This is where Montessori or Steiner education might come into their own to help these children through this difficult stage. After the primary stage, Crystals should have a strong foundation and should be able to deal with their peer-group, but the primary stage will be difficult for many Crystals. Some people may be reluctant to acknowledge that systems of education like Steiner and Montessori, that were set up many decades ago, can be that effective, but the point is that they were set up by beings who were far in advance of their time.

Joanna: What are the common misconceptions that are likely to arise about Crystal Children?

Alariel: One misconception is that all Crystals will be brilliantly academic, and be able to pass examinations with ease. Crystals will all be highly intelligent, but that intelligence will manifest in many ways, and sensitive feeling and intuition are as likely as any academic gift.

Crystals will not, of course, all be little angels, especially when they are going through all the usual emotional process of growing up. Indeed their imaginative abilities may cause them to make chaos in highly creative ways that might never occur to the average Original!

Another misconception is that a Crystal Child can never be willful. Crystals come in knowing a great deal, and if they know their parents are wrong about something, a certain amount of willfulness can come into play.

There is another misconception that all Crystals will respond to the Mother energy and to nature. Those who come from star systems where the Universal Mother is respected will certainly do so. But they will be coming in from a variety of star systems, and some of these are not so Mother-energy oriented.

Joanna: How would you sum up the Crystals as a whole?

Alariel: I would say that they all share one thing – a great lightness of being. Your galaxy and your solar system are stepping up into lighter vibrations, so lightness of being is exactly what is needed on the Earth now. This is the hallmark of all Crystals. A light touch, a certain lightness of consciousness and a wish to avoid heavy conditions, heavy foods, heavy systems and heavy overbearing people. They just regard heavy people and heavy conditions as dysfunctional and unsustainable in the long run, so they instinctively avoid them.

Joanna: Will Crystal Children avoid arguments?

Alariel: Yes, absolutely. Crystals will state what they believe in, but they will not argue to defend those beliefs. They regard argument as a form of verbal combat, and they simply refuse to go into combat mode. Many Originals, used to hearing people argue their case and stand up for their beliefs, will not understand this, and indeed the attitude of the Crystals may annoy them. They will assume that the Crystals are not serious about their beliefs, but they would be wrong about that. Crystals simply choose not to argue with people. If other people accept their beliefs, that's fine, but if they don't, that's also fine, as far as the Crystals are concerned.

Another important aspect about Crystal Children is that they don't compete. They are happy to excel at the exercising of some gift or talent, but they don't regard gifts as in any way competitive. They will not understand the natural human tendency amongst Originals to compete with one another. This will tend to make Crystals very poor sportsmen or sportswomen. Once they have seen a game and understood the rules, a Crystal will see little point in repeating the same game endlessly. They are much more likely to start evolving another game with a different set of rules! This will madden the Originals, who love doing the same things, but doing them better and better each time. A Crystal is just not built like that, and Crystals generally are not interested in competing.

So the principle here is that Crystal Children don't compete and will not argue, something that may lead some Originals to conclude that they lack will-power and determination. This is absolutely untrue of Crystals, who just come from very different and more civilized cultures. But these qualities will lead to much misunderstanding on the part of the Originals.

Joanna: Some authors are saying that the great majority of Crystal Children come from Orion. Could you comment on this please?

Alariel: Many Crystal Children will come through the portal of Orion, but that does not mean they originate in the Orion system. They are drawn from several galaxies because the special needs of the Earth at this time has attracted volunteers from a large number of advanced star civilizations. This is the chance for many advanced star beings to contribute to the Triumph of the Light in your galaxy, and many are volunteering to help humanity in this way.

Joanna: It's going to be quite challenging for some parents to treat the Crystals just as children if they come in with such knowing and such remarkable gifts.

Alariel: Yes, that is true. There is a balance to be struck here. While it is important to recognize the advanced consciousness of Crystal Children, you should not separate them so much in your minds that they become either incomprehensible and scary aliens or icon figures of a new cult. Neither fear nor undue reverence should distort your consciousness in dealing with the Crystal Children. They are simply advanced human beings, so treat them as such. Relate to them as advanced humans, and honor their advancement, which is after all, the advancement which all human beings will soon enjoy. Demonizing or deifying them will make it almost impossible for them to do their work in helping humanity move forward, so it is in everyone's interest to avoid these two extremes.

Joanna: Will most of the Crystals be capable of telepathy?

Alariel: Many Crystals will be telepathic, but not every single one of them. Crystals can communicate in broadly telepathic ways, some of which are not telepathy as you might understand it. These ways are light and subtle, often using visual imagery or imagery combined with words transmitted at very high speeds. This kind of communication might seem to you to be the result of a "hyped-up" or tense consciousness, although to the Crystals, it would seem to be a relaxed, controlled and easy process. Many Crystals just operate, especially at the telepathic level, at what seems to you to be prodigious speed. If you keep tuning in to them, they'll teach you how to adapt to their subtle methods of telepathic signaling.

They can signal much faster than anyone can talk, so relax and try to adapt to this new mode of communication. If you can adapt to it, it can raise the vibrational level and expand consciousness in ways that are beyond your ability to imagine. Being able to communicate in words has served human beings well for many centuries, but now you're entering areas of consciousness where the slow speed of verbal communication is starting to impede your progress. Let go of the slow linear patterns of speech and watch how your consciousness can open and develop in new ways.

Joanna: What other gifts do the Crystal Children bring to us?

Alariel: One of the great gifts of the Crystal Children is to encourage you to go beyond the present limits of your consciousness. Your consciousness limits you in many ways, but one of the most important of these is the way it limits and restricts your future. Your consciousness creates a tunnel out of your past experiences and continues that tunnel through your present awareness. Out of this tunnel of what is probable, your mind projects forward to construct your future, but the tunnel is constrained and limited, so it falls far short of what you could really be and do in that future.

The Crystal Children invite you to step out of the tunnel, to move from the probable to the limitless possible, to envision a far more wonderful future for yourself than you can presently imagine. By helping you to do that, they liberate you from some of the effects of your consciousness, and open a doorway to a future of infinite possibilities.

202

Joanna: So they are helping us to let go of our past?

Alariel: Yes, and the effects that past is having on your present and your future. Most human beings are trying to construct their present as a continuation of their past. Crystal Children have no interest in the past. By being here and now in a very focused and open way, they can construct a path to the possible future that is not past-related at all, but instead represents a new start for humanity.

Have you every wondered what life would be like without a past? What life would be like if everyone on your planet started each day with a clean slate, unburdened by past memories, bitterness, suspicion and prejudice? Well, Crystal Children can live like that, and they are challenging you to leave the past behind and become the Architects of a New Dawn.

Joanna: Will part of that New Dawn be a rethinking of teaching methods? Will Crystal Children change the pattern of education as we know it today?

Alariel: Yes, in time. In those areas where large numbers of Crystal Children are born and whole classes are made up entirely of Crystals, a radical rethink of teaching methods will be required. Let me give you a picture of what this Education of the Future may look like.

Before the beginning of each term, the main teacher for the class will meet with the pupils to discuss that section of the curriculum which has been allocated for this term. Because Crystal Children have the ability to operate at the level of conceptual thought, they will consider, at that level, the material which needs mastering. The class will decide how much time will be needed for this amount of material, and how it should be presented to make it easy to absorb.

Teaching then proceeds, helped along through some tutoring by fellow-pupils, so that the whole class moves forward together. The required material is taught and absorbed during the agreed time and the term finishes on schedule.

Here the pupils are not only fully involved in the educational process, but effectively in control of it because they decide the method of presentation and the speed of learning, and hence the length of the term. Yet the outcome pleases everyone. The teachers are pleased that the set material for the term has been mastered by all the pupils. No one has lagged behind, and no special coaching by teachers has been required.

The pupils are pleased because they've had an interesting term followed by a longer-than-average holiday during which they spent time with their friends. And because the learning process has been handled in this way, with the pupils taking responsibility for helping each other to absorb the knowledge, the cohesion and comradeship within the class has been strengthened.

Although the most progressive education methods now available – notably Montessori – contain some of these elements, the whole package described here is unique within the modern era. It is true that the high peaks of education in Lemuria and Golden Atlantis present some parallels, but nothing as advanced as this has been seen since the fall of Atlantis.

Comment by Joanna on the education of the future: I found Alariel's picture of future education most interesting as I see many echoes here of the Montessori method. Dr. Montessori believed that the early years from birth to six are the time when the child has the greatest openness to learn, and the greatest thirst for knowledge. During these years, children are particularly receptive to stimuli, and are encouraged to use all their senses. Maria Montessori developed her own teaching aids and a whole range of activities to take advantage of this "sensitive period". Montessori education focuses on six core areas of learning: practical life, the senses, language, mathematics, culture and creative activities.

In Montessori Pre-Primary and Primary levels, the children learn at their own pace and own level. There is such a difference in abilities when a child first comes to school, so the slower ones are catered for, but the more able can be stretched and kept engaged. There is no judgment involved. If a child is slow with his reading, for example, the other children will help and it becomes a co-operative effort.

There is no testing in Montessori, but in many State education systems there is early testing, sometimes as young as seven or eight. I feel this is far too young to put this burden on a child. We should allow them their childhood. Children actually love to learn and they learn best by play, seeing and doing, and there is plenty of that in a Montessori school.

All the Montessori equipment is inter-related and self-correcting. If a child makes a mistake, it is the teacher's fault, as she has either shown the child before he is ready, or she has not explained it clearly enough. There is great respect for the child, and the system is based on the drawing out of the child, rather than trying to cram information in. It is so important in the early years not to destroy confidence, but to build self esteem.

The Montessori practice of the "Silence Game" is the beginning of simple meditation. I have seen this meditation help a small boy deal with, for the first time, his difficult feelings after his father's death. He was helped to come to terms with these feelings by the compassion and understanding shown by his fellow classmates.

It is altogether a very holistic system.

26

Understanding the New Children

by Jennifer Crews

Within the past 20 years, different generations of children have entered our world with amazing new characteristics. They have become recognized as the New Children. As a Child Intuitive in professional practice with a background in pediatric speech language pathology, I have had the opportunity to get to know many of these children and their families over the course of 13 years. I witnessed the wide variety of diagnoses that were tossed around in the medical and educational fields in the hope of labeling and treating these children. These labels include sensory integration disorder, autism spectrum disorder, attention deficit disorder, and pervasive developmental disorder, along with others.

This rampant labeling of children has been an attempt to help parents and professionals understand different intervention techniques and approaches. In the intuitive profession, different kinds of labels are currently being adopted, including such terms as Indigo, Crystal, and Rainbow children. Again these names summarize a grouping of characteristics applicable to certain children. I choose to follow and embrace a dramatically different and new perspective – a new paradigm regarding these children, and how we can better honor them and welcome them into our society.

Although one out of every 150 children is currently being labeled with autism spectrum disorder, there is no epidemic occurring around Autism. What is really happening is a human evolution. All of these unique children are coming into our world to teach a new way of perceiving our environment, our worlds, and how to communicate within them. The new children are pioneers in new methods of communication, intuitive and telepathic methods which will eventually replace verbal communication.

I know there are many strategies and resources currently linked with each of the labels used to diagnose children today, but I offer a simpler and more effective paradigm that will change the way you view your child. All of these children who fall under every category mentioned earlier, have two things in common that most professionals and parents are not recognizing:

1. They see, interact, feel and connect with ENERGY FIRST.
2. They see, interact, feel and connect with the PHYSICAL WORLD SECOND.

It's that simple. Unfortunately, most professionals and parents have not been taught to understand energy and the energetic world that surrounds us and makes up our environment. Everyone continues to try and find answers in the physical world to assist these children, but this is just not effective. It is through energy awareness that we will learn to relate to the new children. If more individuals understood the energetic world, then they would know how to connect with these children and truly understand them. These new children are teaching us about energy, and about communication with the invisible world. They are teaching us about dimensions that cannot be seen directly at the physical level. They are also teaching us about love and heart energy.

The new children have ten subtle systems which contribute to their individual well-being when all ten systems are working in harmony:

1. Immune
2. Digestive
3. Nervous/Regulatory
4. Relational
5. Self Expression/Communication
6. Body Rhythm Cycles
7. Perceptional
8. Energy Awareness
9. Grid Awareness
10. Nature Connection

When one or more of these systems is out of balance, blocked, disrupted or disturbed, the child will communicate through a response or a reaction to his or her environment. Many in the traditional educational and medical fields refer to these forms of communication as "behaviors," but I do not. I feel that, for all children, a behavior is merely a form of communication. They may not be aware of what is disturbing them, or causing misalignment in one or more of their ten systems, but they are communicating a message. It is our job to become the interpreters of this message.

The difficulty is that most professionals and parents try to interpret the communication from a physical perspective. Instead, we need to shift our approach and start interpreting their communications from an energy perspective, being aware that the physical world and the energy world are extensions of each other. The new children are built very differently from the rest of us. They have entered this world with new wiring within all the familiar systems, as well as collectively creating several new systems. This is an entirely natural process of human evolution. In order to support and promote the well-being of these children, it is necessary for parents and professionals to understand the ten systems that are an integral aspect of each child:

1.   The Immune System reflects the current state of health, and the ability to maintain health and fight off foreign bodies. The new children are either very fragile and hyper-sensitive, with vulnerable immune systems, or extremely strong, with solid and resilient constitutions. I have yet to observe any new children that have immune systems falling in between these two extremes. Their immune systems are triggered by the emotional state of their family, community and nation, as well as the state of the world. They energetically feel and absorb influences from all these sources, and their immune systems respond accordingly. This is an important awareness for all parents and professionals to reflect upon. Because of their highly developed sensitivity, we have a much greater impact on the new children than we would on the average child. That is why it is so vital for you to know yourself and heal your emotional wounds.

2.   Digestive System: Most of the new children are aware of what their bodies can and cannot handle. They naturally avoid certain foods that do not work for them. This innate awareness typically starts at a very early age. You will hear families say, "Yes, she does not eat dairy at all – she just avoids it." The child already knows that it does not feel good in her body. They have their own regulatory digestive system that they honor and understand. On many occasions, I will meet children that already know all of their allergies. They have a built-in barometer that prevents them from eating anything that will not make them feel good. It is important to understand and listen to these new children – they really do know their own bodies.

3.   The Nervous System is the most vital system for the new children. Most "acting out" is directly correlated with a disturbance in the child's nervous system. The nervous systems of the new children are hypersensitive to all

210

environmental stimuli. The best way to describe it is to say that they have more nerves throughout their bodies than you or I. This is true energetically, but may not be reflected at the physical level. Their nervous system, under an x-ray, may look the same as ours, but it is much more sensitive to the impact of sight, sound, taste, touch and smell. When they become overloaded, their nervous system reacts, trying to bring itself back into balance. I have learned that every child is different, and I have seen hundreds of ways these children attempt to regulate their nervous system. What is important to recognize is that this system is strongly affected by energy, as well as the physical world, and it plays a big role in the child's overall well-being.

4. The Relational System is how the child observes and perceives the people around him or her based on the energy and vibrational quality of a person. These children see right through you. They can tell if what you are saying actually matches the vibration you are sending out, and they can sense people's intentions and motives. They can assess a person or a situation vibrationally and energetically. This is a huge gift they bring to this world, but it is also the reason why so many new children are struggling in traditional schools. If a teacher is not in full integrity, these children will see right through them, and challenge them.

The old patterns of teaching are not in alignment with the new children. This gift of a highly-tuned relational system requires parents and teachers to be in integrity, and be authentic within themselves as well as with others. These children can see deception, bribery and distraction quite acutely, and it is important to honor this. If they are uncomfortable around somebody or some situation, it is their relational system telling them to pay attention, and this can be astoundingly accurate.

5. Self Expression and Communication play a significant role in the well-being of each child. The traditional approach of using verbal communication – "Tell us how you feel" – will not apply to the new children. Some of them may not talk at all and will be labeled nonverbal. Others will only say a few words or short phrases, or repeat what others are saying. The new children have their own unique forms of communication and self expression, often involving intuition and energetic telepathy. It is these new communication methods which will eventually replace verbal patterns and become the most widely accepted forms of communication. However, currently we are conditioned to believe that verbal communication is the only comprehensive and effective form, and this belief limits these new children.

Verbal expression is only one way of sharing information. Other forms of communication and full self expression include the visual arts, dance, body movement, music and rhythm. And what about energetic communication? Or telepathy? Or telekinetic communication: the moving of objects across a room without touching them? And have you thought about communicating with different dimensions or with the invisible world?

6. Each one of us has a particular Body Rhythm Cycle. My body cycle reminds me when my blood sugar is running low and I need to eat a sustaining meal. It also prompts me when I need alone time away from other people and energies. The new children recognize their body cycle and they adhere to it tenaciously, although many people perceive this as stubborn or lazy or self-focused. We just do not respect or listen closely enough to be able to recognize this natural body rhythm cycle in the children.

Pay attention to the body cycle of your child. When are they most productive? When do they need space and alone time? Learn your child's cycle and honor it. You can work within their cycle, and you'll be amazed how much easier your relationship will flow if you do this.

7. The Perceptional System is directly related to the senses. The new children require integration of all their senses to feel safe and good within their bodies. They typically have one or more senses that are more powerful and heightened compared to you or I. One child might see the grains of wood in a kitchen table, while another may hear a spider crawling in the corner of a room, or the hum of street lights in a parking lot. They also have an awareness that goes beyond the traditional five senses to encompass vibrational knowing, intuitive knowing, and energy awareness.

8. Energy Awareness is the feeling, sensing and acute knowing of energy that is invisible. This energy has a wide variety of different vibrational qualities and underpins everything that exists in the physical world. The new children understand that everything is a symbol representing something greater than itself. They know for example that 3 has an energy quality that can give access to much more information than the mere number 3 would suggest. Through energy awareness, some new children can understand and communicate with animals. Others can move objects across a room by pushing and moving the invisible energy. It is important to recognize that many of the new children will be geniuses in understanding and using energy.

9. Grid Awareness is an extension of energy awareness. The planet is covered with an energetic grid, like a subtle and invisible kind of global internet which connects us all. The new children who persevere with lining up their trains and toys, and then lie on the floor to follow the line they have created, are mimicking the planetary grid. They feel the grid and sometimes they see it. Some even use it to communicate

with children on the other side of the world. The grid plays a dominant role in their emotional states because they feel what is happening all over the world through being connected to the grid.

10. Nature Connection promotes peace, groundedness, and contentment for the new children. Their inner wisdom tells them that nature is an essential aspect of ourselves, and the more we tune in to nature, the stronger we become in loving ourselves and others. I have observed that every new child I meet is innately and deeply connected with one of the main elements. Water, wood, fire, air and earth are the elements I have witnessed so far.

Determine which element your child resonates with most and you have found the tool to help calm them and bring them comfort. Surround them with that element. If you can't determine which element is strongest, expose them to nature as much as possible. All nine of their other systems will then come quickly into balance and their overall well-being will improve. I encourage water fountains and plants in bedrooms. I have found this has helped a significant number of the new children I have met.

Awareness of the ten systems is fundamental in promoting balance, peace and overall well-being in the new children. Dedicate yourself to becoming attentive to the role these ten systems play in the lives of your children and the children around you. Recognition and appreciation of how these ten systems affect your child will create a better understanding of who they are and what they are teaching. Contribute to the well-being of the new children by learning and becoming aware of energy and of your self. This is the greatest gift you can give to every child.

(NOTE: This contribution by Jennifer Crews M.A. first appeared in a longer form in 2008 in *Children of the New Earth* (www.childrenofthenewearth.com). This Chapter is (c) Copyright 2008 Intuitive Teachings, LLC.)

Jennifer Crews is the founder of Intuitive Teachings, an enterprise offering individual, group and teleseminar teaching sessions on a range of topics including the Art of Intuition, the New Children, Energy Management and Multidimensional Living. She is a Child Intuitive, Certified Spiritual Teacher, Visionary Author and Educator dedicated to honoring the essence of children and adults worldwide.

Jennifer writes: I have devoted my life to teaching parents and professionals about intuition and energy to assist in understanding themselves and the new children. I am more than happy to share that knowledge and assist you to diving deeper into energy awareness, your personal intuition, and understanding your child. I look forward to supporting you as you choose to see yourself and your children from a new paradigm and making a difference in their lives.

You can contact Jennifer Crews through her website:

www.intuitiveteachings.com.

Part Eight:

A New Dawn

The New World comes to us in many ways:
it lives in the soaring of the eagle-soul,
and in moments touched by the grace of the Spirit.
Look for it in the laughter of the children,
and see it shining in the eyes
of those who live their lives
as a rainbow of possibilities.

Stuart Wilson

27

Towards a New World

We had received a vast amount of information from Alariel, and this had opened up many areas of understanding, some of these being entirely new to us. Yet even when we reached this point, there remained some key questions which we still wanted to explore.

One of these questions concerned the Grail, which is usually referred to as the cup used by Jeshua at the Last Supper. However, the Grail has become the focus of many myths and legends over the centuries, and the bestseller *The Holy Blood and the Holy Grail* has lifted the debate onto another level. After all this controversy, we wanted to consult Alariel in order to get his perception of the Grail and its significance.

Joanna: Some people associate the Grail with Mary Magdalene. Could you comment on this please?

Alariel: The symbolism of the Grail is vast, but we would be happy to share our perspective with you. On one level, the Grail can be seen as the Mystery School working through the Temple of Isis in Alexandria, which provided a structure, a container – a "cup," if you wish to call it that – into which the Initiates of Love and Light could pour their loving service. This Mystery School was in many ways one of the highest, purest and most effective practical expressions of Melchizedek wisdom upon this planet, and its benevolent influence still endures.

On another level, the Grail can be seen as the bloodline reaching from Mary Magdalene down to the present day, a lineage which has provided physical vehicles for a number of Workers in the Light, especially those souls who had experienced lives as Priestesses of Isis. Through Mary, the energy and wisdom of the Isis tradition of Love and Light did not disappear when the temple of Isis faded into history, but continued in the life and work of all those who have been inspired by it over the centuries. For this reason, we regard Mary Magdalene as the overlighting presence sustaining the Grail, and in a symbolic sense, her higher self can be seen as the Angel of the Grail.

On a still deeper level, the Grail can be interpreted as the Vortex of Cosmic Peace and Unconditional Love which the work of Jeshua and Mary Magdalene established upon the Earth. This new blend of energies gave all subsequent aspirants the opportunity to balance Peace and Love within the heart and go forward into realization and ascension in a much more direct way than was practiced in the ancient Mystery Schools.

Comment by Stuart: Alariel's statement here gave us one more opportunity to explore the Melchizedek teachings, an area already researched in some depth through writing our first book, *The Essenes, Children of the Light.*

The session continues:

Joanna: You speak of the Mystery School at Alexandria as one of the highest expressions of Melchizedek wisdom upon the Earth. What aspect of the Melchizedek wisdom do you find most profound?

Alariel: Their teaching on balance. The Melchizedeks realized that balance was central to the nature of the Universe, due to their clear perception of Father-Mother God. They also saw that the principle of balance is reflected down through all the levels of being. Those who thoroughly understand the principle of balance would never, for example, undervalue the Goddess aspect of the Divine, or the power and importance of feminine wisdom.

The Melchizedeks saw balance as being vital, not only to a whole civilization, but to all levels within a single being. For life to be lived to the full, it needs to be lived in a balanced way, so that each aspect of the individual is respected and given the time and attention required for full expression. They saw health and wholeness flowing naturally from a state of being in which all aspects of a person are in balance. And they said that any structure or society based upon imbalance was essentially dysfunctional and unsustainable.

The Melchizedeks also regarded balance as linked with, and leading to, harmony, which they recognized as the Law of Laws, and the state towards which the whole Universe constantly moved. Harmony, they said, is the key to understanding all the other Laws. Hence they saw Karma, for example, as essentially a moving back into balance and harmony, an attempt by the Universe to restore a state of balance.

Those who, like Jeshua, spent time with Melchizedek teachers absorbing their wisdom always emphasized the need for balance as a central component in life. That is why he set up his system of discipleship in a balanced way, each circle of male disciples being balanced by a female counterpart. Thus the fundamental nature of the Universe was reflected in the structure of his teaching system.

Joanna: If balance is so vital, is imbalance always dangerous?

Alariel: It almost always leads to some kind of dysfunction in an individual or in society as a whole. For example, a culture based on any extreme form of patriarchy might come close

221

to destroying its planetary environment. Those who do not respect their planetary Mother are very likely to pollute and injure her, because nothing in their belief system will hold them back. Any extreme patriarchal culture will also tend to produce conflict and suffering because the co-operative, loving and forgiving qualities are all functions of the Divine Feminine, which will be deliberately marginalized in this type of culture.

Let us be clear about this: an extreme matriarchal culture also has its problems, and will lead to other forms of dysfunctionality, including a lack of structure and intellectual rigor. But at least, those who believe in matriarchy will be in no danger of destroying their own planet.

So what we are advocating is a balanced belief system, in other words, a belief in Father-Mother God.

Joanna: The whole idea of patriarchy does seem to be widely questioned now, and is no longer accepted as the natural order of things.

Alariel: In the West, you are experiencing a time of re-evaluating and rebalancing. What started as a rebalancing within relationships is now culminating in a rebalancing of your whole belief system. The increasing interest in the Sacred Feminine, the female disciples of Jeshua, and the role played by Mary Magdalene, are all part of this rebalancing process.

Rebalancing your belief system is an essential precondition for moving out of your past limitations and into the very different energy conditions of the New World, a World in which all aspects of the Divine will be valued.

The whole process of transformation and rising in consciousness, supported by the New Children, will lay the foundations for this New World. New horizons will open up, including the possibility of living in a post-conflict, post-competitive world in which collaboration and forgiveness replace the destructive patterns of your past.

222

This is the New Dawn that human beings have longed for, the new beginning that all your efforts have brought forth.

This is the New World in which you are no longer the dependent children of Creation, but spiritually-adult Beings, standing in the Light of your own Consciousness.

28

The New Consciousness

Joanna: What do you see as the most useful thing that angels can do now to help humanity at this stage of our development?

Alariel: To help you let go of your past and all the heaviness of the old perception of things, the rigidities of the old order. You are constantly being challenged to expand your awareness and reach out into new frequencies of consciousness, new perspectives of truth, new possibilities of being.

You have been accustomed to looking outside of yourselves for guidance, reassurance, ultimately for authorization and authority. Now you are entering a new phase where the challenge is to receive your guidance from within.

The Spirit works through manifesting in your life as much Light as you can handle. The Light provides the fire of transformation, the flames in which all that is NOT Light within you will be consumed. Welcome this fire when it comes, for the fire is your friend. By sacrificing all your heaviness, all your negativity, all your fears and doubts and limitations into this flame you are reborn as a lighter, purer, subtler Being. A Being who resonates with the frequencies of Light.

We cannot tell you how great a change this will bring into your lives. It will be like moving from being a docile and obedient child to being an independent and responsible adult. Spiritually, humanity is waking up and moving out of the child stage of dependence upon external authority and into the stage of spiritual empowerment.

And this shift in the very nature of your being is also a shift out of your heavy and regimented past and into a much lighter and more flexible consciousness. To soar up into the new frequencies of being that await you, it will be necessary for your consciousness to become infinitely more subtle and flexible and open to new possibilities and creative solutions. You cannot step into your future wearing the heavy hob-nail boots of your grandfathers – what are needed now are light and agile dancing shoes!

To date, you have marched and plodded from one generation to the next, but it is time to spread your wings and soar upwards into the New World, and all the new possibilities that lie before you. So think about how heavy – or light – your consciousness has been today, how heavy it was yesterday and how light and joyful it will be tomorrow. Everything around you is changing and evolving, and your consciousness needs to change and evolve too. And when you get used to the New Consciousness, you will find its lightness easy and elegant, like a pebble skimming across the waves.

The New World will be based upon co-operation rather than competition, sharing rather than accumulating, Oneness rather than separation. These are big changes compared to the way most human beings now live, and these changes will bring big challenges as part of the process of realignment. Moving into the New World is made much easier if you let go of the heaviness, the fear, the anger, the bitterness, the hatred, the suffering: everything that is not light and of the Light. If you do that, you will find your consciousness will change more quickly and more easily from day to day, automatically leaving all that is heavy behind and moving naturally towards all that is light: light

friends, light foods, light ideas and light ways of living.
Eventually, the heavy will just seem absurd and irrelevant to
you – it will pass you by, for in your New Consciousness,
only the Light will find a home.

Joanna: Is there any practical technique that can help us move
into this New Consciousness?

Alariel: Yes, there is. As you are essentially Spirit, essentially
Light, we can recommend this powerful meditation that will
support your transformational process:

Either lie down, or sit in a chair, or sit on the floor in a
cross-legged or half-lotus posture, whichever is comfortable
for you. Close your eyes, center yourself, and breathe
deeply. Either say aloud or think these words:

I surrender to the Spirit,
I surrender to the Light.

I surrender to the Spirit,
I surrender to the Light.

I surrender to the Spirit,
I surrender to the Light.

I AM Light, I AM Light, I AM Light.

When you say or think these words, send them out like
a pulse into the Universe and then tune in to your physical
sensations and your feelings. As each wave goes out, the
response will change and evolve, and it may bring you a
glimpse of joy and intense bliss. Stay within this resonance
of bliss and let it wash over you like the ocean for as long as
you wish. Then breathe deeply and open your eyes.

Let the Light expand within you till it fills your whole being.

Let the Light become your teacher and let it gently change and transform you to appropriate patterns and frequencies as you move steadily towards Oneness.

The channels of the Light bring you energy and information to nurture your growth, and weave you ever more lovingly into the Web of Light which is the Universe.

29

The Challenge of Oneness

Joanna: What is the biggest challenge that you see ahead for us?
Alariel: To focus on Oneness, and on the need to change human society so that it reflects Oneness. From our perspective, Oneness is the only true reality, and all the apparent fragmentation of life on Earth is an illusion. The illusion lies in the apparent separation of each being, its ability to stand alone in isolation from all other beings. Your scientists are now discovering that all living beings are much more closely connected than you have thought. You all exist in a continuum of consciousness and energy, and you could not cut yourself off from this shared life-system and still exist.

That knowledge is the beginning of respect. Living on planet Earth is very much about learning respect. Respect for all life-forms, all traditions and cultures, however strange they may seem to be. We see changes in this direction in many levels of human consciousness, and many little movements away from the traditional view of outsiders as rivals or adversaries. Despite continuing areas of chaos and conflict, humanity is exploring unity in a way that would have been unthinkable only a generation ago. International lines of communication and structures of co-operation are evolving into the ability to think and act globally, a total human response to the greatest human need.

So that this collaboration can work effectively, you are having to let go of the heaviness of your battle-scarred past, and consign your fears and suspicions to the rubbish-heap of history. You are even starting to go beyond greed and learning to live in a sustainable way which does not do violence to this planet. And you are discovering that the only way for anyone to win in the long term, is for everyone to win, including the Earth.

The whole of this planet, which you have been studying as a unified energy-system, is now emerging into your awareness as a unified consciousness-system. More than that, you are beginning to understand that energy and consciousness are not two separate things, but one thing. And together they make up a continuous and unbroken web of being:

One Energy and Consciousness in all that is, and all existence as one Web of Life.

It is quite a leap of understanding to grasp that energy and consciousness are different frequencies of one thing. Your physicists are only just in the earliest stages of beginning to grapple with this. And the whole of your science is now moving forward into subtle and challenging areas. The holistic and integrative vision pioneered by your philosophers is now becoming the everyday reality of your scientists as they study the human and planetary ends of this vast continuum, and its subtle and life-sustaining links and connections.

Unity is starting to look less like an impossible dream and more like a description of the scientific reality of things, and a formula for personal and planetary survival. And because of all of this you are beginning to expand your awareness, and reach out into new possibilities of being. All this is transforming you in ways which your grandparents could not even begin to understand. And the more you can flow with this energy and attune to Unity Consciousness, the

230

faster you will bring reconciliation into your divided world.

Part of your journey into Oneness is a letting go of your past. Try not to hold a fixed position on anything or anyone. However keenly you feel the rights and wrongs of a particular situation, this may change with time:

> *Yesterday's reviled terrorist leader*
> *becomes today's accepted political negotiator*
> *and tomorrow's honored statesman.*

Time moves on, people change and the perception of them changes too. Always allow for that change by keeping an open mind on everything and everyone.

Hold onto nothing and resist nothing. That way you keep your energy focused on the Here and Now, and your consciousness remains forever young. You also avoid stress, one major cause of which is a failure to let go. Let life flow through you, and acknowledge and accept whatever life presents to you today.

Be aware, accept, let go and move on.

By doing this, you keep in the flow of Oneness and do not pull yourself out of the stream into separation and isolation. These qualities are part of the long arc leading to rigidity and death. By choosing the path of flow, the path of Oneness, you choose the path of life. In doing that, you automatically move towards the point of equilibrium, the focus of balance.

In equilibrium, all the drama of the world falls away, all the struggling and judging, all the heartache and the hurt. Here only Love and Light are real, and all else blows away upon the wind. In this state, you understand that everything is perfect, not in the sense of being equally good, but in the

231

realization that the perfect balance of things teaches you Love and helps you to move towards the Light.

Joanna: Much of what you say about Oneness has resonances with modern physics, especially quantum physics. This seems to have developed very quickly into some quite subtle and holistic areas.

Alariel: Yes, and the pace of development is increasing all the time. Your scientists are now embracing the possibility of a multidimensional universe as the only way that they can get the mathematics to work. Mathematics do not lie, but sometimes they demand that you change your ideas if they are too rigid and limiting.

This realignment and expansion of consciousness comes at a vital time for you. You live in a divided and dangerous world where it is all too easy to forget about Oneness and forgiveness, and start to think in terms of punishment and revenge. Yet despite that, it is still true that solutions based upon violence divide, whilst those based upon forgiveness unite.

Joanna: Is it necessary for the persecutor to repent and show remorse before complete forgiveness by the victim is possible?

Alariel: No. Jeshua did not say, "Stand ready to forgive your enemy as soon as he repents." Instead, his message was simply to forgive your enemy. Forgiveness can occur at any time, and as soon as you have forgiven someone, you have released yourself from the energetic connection between you. By forgiving, you reject any kind of separation and affirm Oneness. Unity Consciousness is a hard lesson to learn, but forgiveness is a vital component in the spiritual growth of an awakening humanity.

Joanna: But Oneness can sometimes be very challenging.

Alariel: Yes. You will be challenged to experience the dramas of this world, and not be pulled in by them; to live surrounded by turbulence and chaos and still hold the vision of Love and

Peace.

In a time of chaos, it is hard to hold both sides equally in the Light, and to send your blessings to all, yet that is exactly what you need to do now. For now your lives are intersecting with the greater process of planetary transformation, and the Inner and Outer worlds are merging into one. Release the heavy energy that locks you into duality and step forward into the Oneness of the heart.

30

Melchizedek and Metatron

When we were researching our first book *The Essenes, Children of the Light*, Alariel revealed a good deal of information about the Melchizedeks and their relationship with the Essenes. Although we understood that the Order of Melchizedek is a service Order of advanced teachers operating in many parts of the galaxy, we still knew very little about the Head of the Order, so we framed a question to cover this:

Joanna: Could you please tell us about the great Being who founded the Melchizedek Order?

Alariel: To understand Melchizedek, it is first necessary to understand his relationship to Metatron. The work of these two great Beings interlocks and neither can be understood in isolation.

There are two main aspects of the Universe: Light (which may also be perceived as energy) and Consciousness. Light creates all the levels of the Universe right down to the physical level. All that you can see (including other beings) are made of Light, crystallized or solidified down till it reaches the physical level.

Consciousness creates the process through which beings of Light evolve spiritually, that evolution giving you the reason for your existence and the arc of your development. Both a rock and the greatest Archangel are made of Light, but the consciousness of the rock exists in potential, whereas the consciousness of the Archangel exists in unfoldment and realization. In vibrational terms, the consciousness of a rock is extremely slow, unorganized and crude, while the consciousness of a great Archangel is fast, structured and refined.

Metatron oversees the energy, the Light aspect of the Universe, creating the Light and the Protocols and Language of Light, while Melchizedek oversees the spiritual education and development of consciousness of all material beings. The development of angelic beings is overseen by Metatron. So, in a way, Metatron provides the physical environment in which spiritual evolution occurs, while Melchizedek nourishes and sustains that evolution in the unfolding of consciousness.

Their work is very different, but together they combine to provide a complete experience for many beings on many levels of development. And the net result of their combined work is to take life at a very slow and primitive stage and enable it to expand in awareness so that what emerges in time are Enlightened Beings.

Comment by Stuart: Both Melchizedek and Metatron are considered to be great Beings who exist beyond the normal constraints of space and time. Some authorities say that Metatron is an Archangel, but as he is considered to be the most powerful of all Archangels, it seems more likely that he is one of the Elohim, the leaders of the angelic host and the architects of Creation.

Most authorities regard Melchizedek as an advanced Star Being, that is, a member of a civilization in some galaxy who has gone through an ascension process and is now a timeless and eternal Being of Light.

The session continues:

236

Joanna: Is the Melchizedek teaching limited to sacred geometry?

Alariel: By no means. It is hard for human beings to grasp the absolute flexibility of the Melchizedek teaching process. When they first contact a civilization, they spend time getting to know what that culture is most interested in, and when they teach, they teach within that parameter of interest. Some examples from Earth history may serve to illustrate this process.

They discovered that the Maya were fascinated by time so they taught them about calendars. They discovered that the Druids were fascinated by the natural world, so they taught them the wisdom of trees and herbs and stars. They discovered that the Greeks were fascinated by line and form, so they taught them about sacred geometry. They discovered that the Jews were fascinated by the contrast of Light and darkness, so they taught them about the struggle between good and evil. They discovered that the Egyptians were fascinated by transformation, so they taught them about ascension.

Amongst all the planets bearing sentient life throughout all the galaxies, they found many different peoples interested in many different things, and whatever that interest was, they talked about it. So they forced their views upon no one, but rather helped everyone to expand the seed of Light that lay dormant in their Consciousness. The Melchizedeks have a little phrase to explain this process. They say, "We always work with the current of the water and the grain of the wood." And that is eminently sensible, for to try to teach a people something that they find dull and boring is a thankless task that the Melchizedeks are much too intelligent to attempt!

Joanna: What do you see as the main purpose of the Melchizedeks here on Earth?

Alariel: Above all, the Melchizedeks are trying to help you achieve your potential as human beings, through helping you to refine your consciousness so that you can rise towards the highest reaches of human awareness. The Melchizedeks are fundamentally relinking all the beings they teach to the Source, by showing them how to access the Truth, the Divine Presence within. This process has the effect of reprogramming the consciousness and aligning that consciousness with the underlying Light-structure of the Universe. This automatically takes the individual away from a selfish and materialistic perception of things and reorients them towards more spiritual goals.

The achieving of the goals that lie along your spiritual path will release great joy within you, and these experiences of joy may be seen as the gifts of the Spirit. That is why the Order of Melchizedek has been described as administering the gifts of the Spirit, although to be more exact, they administer the developmental process which enables the gifts of the Spirit to come into your lives.

31

The Technology of Light

As the session with Ingrid had such a real connection with the new energies coming in, the New Children and the New World, we asked Alariel to comment on it.

Alariel: What we are considering here is the Technology of Light. We know this is difficult for many human beings to understand because they are thinking of "light" with a small "l," the common light of star systems, but this is "Light" with a capital "L" – a powerful spiritual energy.

The Technology of Light, originated and structured by Metatron and applied in the development of consciousness by Melchizedek teachers throughout the Universe, is a key factor in spiritual growth and transformation. The unfolding and development of consciousness depends upon this Technology of Light. There are a whole series of techniques, processes and activations which apply the energy of Light to human consciousness to assist in its unfolding.

The energy of Light and of Unconditional Love work together in the process of spiritual unfoldment. If you consider how this combined energy of Light and Love was brought to this planet, there are three main stages in that process:

1. During the Atlantean era, the spiritual leaders at that time began to focus this energy, making it accessible to highly trained Initiates in the temple systems of Atlantis.

2.   Jeshua in Israel anchored this energy through his collaboration with Mary Magdalene, and through the initiatory process of the crucifixion. That process sent a great vertical shaft of this energy down into the Earth, completing the anchoring, and stabilizing this energy into the energy matrix of this planet. Once that had been done, this energy became accessible to anyone who was open to a process of transformation focused through the heart center.

3.   The Crystal Children will circulate this energy out into the world, bringing it into the consciousness and experience of all people of goodwill. This will make it universally accessible in a way that was not possible in the vibrational conditions of two thousand years ago.

Each of these three steps of Focusing, Anchoring and Circulating is a vital link in the chain, and together they prepare human beings for the great adventure of transformation and rapid spiritual growth.

And this whole process of rapid growth and ascension is supported by a system of Light Technology. The Technology of Light works out in practical ways through a complex and integrated system of geometry. The encodements which open "gateways" to the multiple levels of consciousness manifest in the form of geometrical patterns. When you bring your energy field into alignment with the geometry of a gateway, this activates the encodement, enabling you to access that level of consciousness.

Other geometries govern the opening of portals or energy vortexes and channels through which energy and information is transmitted across the Universe. The link between energy, geometry, Light and consciousness is a powerful one. As you move into the New World, this Technology of Light will be much better understood. The Crystal Children in particular are not only ready for this Technology of Light, they will be your best teachers on this subject. Many of them come from advanced civilizations where the Technology of Light has been taught, understood and applied for centuries.

As we have already indicated, the Crystal Children will be able to signal much faster than any verbal communication, and part of this signaling will be an exchange of geometrics, and a subtle range of colors that lie outside the normal human experience. To understand the full significance of these geometrics, it is important to realize that they are not confined to static designs, but involve fluid processes moving through a series of developing patterns.

Comment by Stuart: One of the best examples we have found of the principle of sacred geometry flowing from one pattern to another is the DVD *Merkabah: Voyage of a Star Seed* (see Further Reading under Hurtak.)

The session continues:

Alariel: You can also observe advanced geometrics communicating with the souls who have come in from distant star systems. Many of the crop circle designs are powerful because they have the ability to activate pre-encoded signals from a person's star system of origin. This is not "ET phoning home," this is more like "home phoning ET." That is, the star system of origin sending a wake-up and activation signal to the ex-ETs who are now having a human experience!

Watch out for ever more creative ways of broadcasting advanced geometrics to the human audience. Every group will receive its own "wake-up" call carried by the appropriate geometrical pattern designed to trigger encodements that have been planted in the subtle sequences of the DNA – those sections of it that haven't been understood yet by your scientists.

It is important to realize that your DNA in its higher sequences contains patterns that go far beyond the level at which most humans now function. These patterns relate to your unfoldment and transformation, and your rising from your present state of being into advanced levels of consciousness.

The whole continuum of geometrics throughout the Universe is connected through a holistic pattern of sequences which links everything together in a single integrated system. The nearest analogy we can make here is with the sequence of keys which underpin the structure of music. Once you know how the keys progress through a series of logical shifts, you can begin to understand the whole system. In the same way, the Technology of Light progresses through geometric sequences to present a holistic system of unfolding consciousness that is both unified in its overall design and yet perfectly adapted to each of the individual stages.

Comment by Stuart: We found this section remarkably clear and significant. It gives a framework within which we can begin to understand Ingrid's experience of working with channels of Light during her life in the Temple of Isis. What Alariel is talking about here is the inner history of humanity, an arc of development extending over many thousands of years. The way that spiritual leaders work to promote this development over such a vast time-scale gives hope for the long term spiritual progress of human beings, despite all the chaos and selfishness that seems to dominate the world.

When our second session with Isabel also started to explore advanced and subtle energies, we asked Alariel for his comments on this information too.

Alariel: Advanced human beings who are working for the Light are connected in subtle ways which the average human would not be able to understand. There is a system of energy and consciousness which connects all the Workers in the Light and links them into a web of telepathic communication. This Web of Light uses geometric patterns to integrate the whole system into a holistic grid, with pulses of energy moving throughout the Web so that this is a two-way process, information flowing down from the center, but also flowing up from each individual. Being linked into this grid will establish a subtle resonance connecting to each of the other Workers in the Light, and drawing them into contact with these people, should they ever meet.

Through using this Web, each Worker in the Light develops what we can only call "antenna" in the form of the ability to sense the presence and significance of any other Lightworker that they encounter, even if they should meet them "accidentally," as you would say. The friendships formed by these chance meetings are of a depth and quality that the average human being could not understand. There is a deep connection at the heart level, and a degree of trust that seems to defy conventional logic. However, when you consider that these "chance meetings" may bring together souls who have been friends and colleagues for many lifetimes, this starts to make more sense.

The subtle nature of this Web of Light connecting all the Lightworkers can only be understood by thinking in multidimensional terms. As each human being evolves in consciousness, there are changes in the DNA structure as the multidimensional levels of DNA begin to activate. This activation produces a resonance pulse, a key-signature which is expressed as a musical note. When you center yourself and tune in to the Light, you automatically send out

243

through the Web your keynote as a pulse of energy of a certain vibration. This keynote attracts the attention of other Workers in the Light whose DNA has evolved to the same level, and whose keynotes are on a similar frequency. That draws them into contact with you as you move through the outer world, so that when they meet you in that world, they meet you as old friends and fellow Workers in the Light whose spiritual evolution parallels yours.

This whole subtle process is going to baffle the average human being who is not part of this Lightworking process, as it seems to defy logic. But those who are capable of thinking in multidimensional ways will find this perfectly reasonable.

Another aspect of this process is the way it expands your ability to respond to geometrical patterns and subtle colors that are pale, shimmering or iridescent. The very subtle colors and moving, flowing geometrics feed you at the soul level and expand your abilities in ways that go beyond your present understanding. These inputs through the Web of Light are preparing you for the work that lies ahead, work that requires a degree of sensitivity that is currently very rare amongst humans. In a sense, these inputs give you a taste of the subtle and liberated life of unfolding consciousness that is to come.

32

Evolution and Design

Here Alariel continues to develop the theme of the last chapter:

Alariel: Unfolding consciousness is paralleled by unfolding and developing geometrics, giving the whole process an essential unity that could not be achieved by any piecemeal design or random combination of elements. Intelligent design, expressed in mathematics and geometrics, governs the whole process of universal creation and unfoldment – a design managed and implemented by the angelic host, and sustained by the Technology of Light.

This system incorporates both physical and spiritual evolution in order to generate the greatest possible diversity of life manifesting in countless star systems across millions of galaxies. This broad sweep of life produces ever more subtle and harmonious forms and expressions of consciousness as each life-wave moves through its natural cycle of development.

*Physical evolution may produce
diversity of form and function,
but only spiritual evolution can produce
diversity of consciousness.*

In the aggregate of all the consciousnesses in all the galaxies, you can begin to glimpse the vastness of

Father-Mother God. This Totality of All That Is continuously develops and evolves, and your human evolution is part of that wider process of development.

You have been the unconscious children of God, but are now becoming conscious leaders of the process of change and spiritual growth. It is time to put away the limiting beliefs and authoritarian values of your earlier history and stand forth as the Empowered and God-illumined Beings that you really are. This is the destiny of an Awakening Humanity, as Creation moves into Co-Creation and the true purpose of the Universe begins to emerge into your understanding.

Though you have achieved much, and traveled far upon your spiritual pilgrimage, the Vastness of your Adventure into Consciousness is only just beginning. You are starting to outgrow the limitations of this small planet, and as your illumined consciousness transcends its boundaries, you become:

> *Masters of all the Laws of Mind and Matter,*
> *Travelers upon the Higher Planes of Being,*
> *Citizens of the Universe.*

This is the real purpose of your lives – not to push out a little way into space, but to explore all the possibilities of consciousness and being. The more you explore the realm of consciousness, the more you transcend the illusion of duality and enter the Reality of Oneness that is your passport to Limitless Being. Through this process, your relationship with your environment changes and you cease to view Nature as something to be conquered. From this new perspective, you will begin to understand how well the Universe has nourished you and provided for your needs. And in this new understanding, you will begin at last to see the greater purpose behind it all.

Originated through intelligent design
and developing through the processes
of physical and spiritual evolution,
the Universe provides an ideal theater
for the subtle play and interplay of consciousness.

Through aligning your lives with this broader
understanding, you will increasingly sense the existence of
a deeper level that restores and nourishes you:

At this level there is nothing to understand,
nothing to remember and nothing to do.

At this level there is no tension or conflict,
for here the Father-energy of Peace
and the Mother-energy of Love
are united in the Mystery of Oneness.

Here there are no questions to ask,
no difficulties to struggle with,
and no burdens to carry.

Here understanding gives way to knowing,
and all your hurts are healed.

Part Nine:
Conclusion

Our lives are rooted in the earth,
and yet they soar and sing
until they touch the stars.

Stuart Wilson

33

Afterword:
Soar and Sing

What started as past life research in a quiet West of England valley has now – through our book *The Essenes, Children of the Light* – gone out into the world and is bringing an ever-widening circle of friends into contact with each other. We feel this networking process is so important as we move through the 2012 experience because it's nice to know that you're not alone in seeing the world in quite a different way!

Now another journey has come to an end, and this second book is ready to go out into the world. We send our best wishes to all our readers, and if you want to contact us please get in touch by email (see the section called "Feedback From Readers"). We'd love to hear from you!

Although the past life sessions remain the core of this book, the whole project was lifted onto a new level through our contact with Alariel. It would have been a much duller and less interesting book without all this input from Alariel, and to him and his angelic team we send our thanks.

What we learned above all through this contact was that angels regard the long-term future of humanity as being positive and hopeful. Drawing upon their optimism, we sense that remarkable events may lie ahead, as we move into a very special and significant time.

This is a time to move into new patterns of living, and new ways of being. A time to awaken and look around us. And a time to spread our wings and reach out into a better future.

Soar and sing!

Glossary

AD/BC: These terms are disliked by many non-Christians and the modern equivalents have been used in this book: CE (Christian Era) and BCE (Before the Christian Era).

Angels: Non-physical Beings who serve Father-Mother God, and who act as "messengers" bringing support, insight and inspiration to humanity.

Ascension: Jewish tradition records the ascension of Enoch and Elijah and (in the non-canonical texts) four other ascensions. Ascension is a process of raising vibration, expanding consciousness and merging with the Light.

Atlantis: The legendary ancient continent which was reputed to cover much of what is now the Atlantic ocean.

Cathars: A movement of independent Christians, inspired by Gnostic ideals, which flourished mainly in southern France and northern Italy between 1140 and 1244 CE. Pope Innocent III initiated a Crusade against the Cathars in 1208, and the movement never recovered from the massacre at Montsegur in 1244 CE.

Dead Sea Scrolls: About 500 mainly Hebrew and Aramaic scrolls (or scroll fragments) discovered from 1947 onwards in the caves of Qumran and in other locations near the Dead Sea.

Druids: The teachers and leaders of the Celtic peoples. The Druids had contact with both the Kaloo and the Essenes.

Elohim: The leaders of the angelic host. These great Angelic Beings are regarded as the architects of Creation.

Essenes: One of the three main groupings within Judaism at the time of Jeshua. (See also Pharisees and Sadducees.)

Etherium Gold: A trace mineral, also called Monatomic Gold, which occurs naturally in ancient mineral deposits. It takes the form of a powder with unusual electromagnetic and superconductive properties.

Gnostics: A movement of free-thinking and independent mystics which emerged in the early years of Christianity. Gnosis is a state of Deep Knowing in which the knower and the known merge and become one.

Israel: Throughout this book, "Israel" has been used rather than the traditional term "Palestine". The Jews have always disliked that term because it comes from a root word meaning "Philistine".

Jeshua benJoseph: The Essene name for Jesus, another form of which is Yeshua. As Jeshua was never called "Jesus" during his lifetime, we have used the original authentic form of his name throughout this book.

Jesus: see Jeshua.

Kabala: see Qabalah.

Kaloo: The last few scattered remnants of the Altantean peoples. They founded the Essene communities, working under the direction of the Order of Melchizedek.

Lemuria: The legendary ancient continent which was reputed to cover much of what is now the Pacific ocean.

Light: Light in the spiritual sense (with a capital "L") is the boundless and eternal Divine Light (the Ain Soph). This is quite distinct from the common light of star systems (with a small "l").

Light Body: Also called the Garment of Light or the Merkabah. This is the Body of Light which is a key to the ascension process: it provides a vehicle of consciousness when eventually form is transcended and the physical body is no longer required.

Melchizedek: A great Star Being who presides over the Order of Melchizedek, a service order of advanced Teachers working on many planetary systems throughout the galaxy.

Messiah: The Jewish savior who was expected to save his people and restore the glory of Israel. Regarded by Jews as a great prophet and a king in the Davidic line.

Metatron: A great Angelic Being who oversees the Light aspect of the Universe, creating the Light and the Protocols and Language of Light.

Mystery Schools: Centers for learning, testing and spiritual growth throughout the ancient world. Their most advanced Initiates reached high levels of consciousness.

Palestine: see Israel.

Pharisees: The rabbinic group which controlled the education system operating through the synagogues. When the Sadducees and the Essenes disappeared, the Pharisaic group was left as the mainstream of modern Judaism.

Qabalah: The mystical core of Judaism, founded on the teachings in the Zohar or *Book of Splendours* and focusing upon the symbolism of the Tree of Life.

Rainbow Consciousness: Also known as Full-Spectrum Consciousness. This is a state of awareness in which all options and possibilities can be seen, because the consciousness is not distorted or diminished by blocks or limitations.

Sadducees: The wealthy land-owning group of Jews who were mainly priests and who controlled the Temple in Jerusalem.

Star Beings: Beings, usually physical in form during some part of their evolution, who populate various civilizations in this galaxy, and in other galaxies. They are sometimes called "ETs" or "extra-terrestrials".

Yeshua: see Jeshua.

Zealots: A group of extremist Jews who saw themselves as Warriors for God, and who focused on an apocalyptic war in which the Romans would be expelled and Israel reclaimed and purified.

Further Reading

We gave a number of Essene sources in the Further Reading section of our book *The Essenes, Children of the Light*, so there is no need to repeat that information here. Instead, we focus on sources that link directly to this book.

Astell, Christine, *Discovering Angels: Wisdom, Healing, Destiny*, Duncan Baird Publishers, London, 2005. A well-written, thorough and beautifully illustrated introduction to the world of angels. (For workshops see www.angellight.co.uk)

Atwater, P .M.H, *Beyond the Indigo Children: The New Children and the Coming of the Fifth World*, Bear & Co. Rochester, VT, 2005. Provides practical help in recognizing and parenting the New Children. One of the few books to grasp the bigger picture and show how the New Children fit into that picture.

Baigent, Michael; Leigh, Richard; and Lincoln, Henry: *The Holy Blood and the Holy Grail*, Arrow Books, London, 1996 (originally published by Jonathan Cape in 1982.) This is the international bestseller which first popularized the controversial ideas surrounding Mary Magdalene.

Brown, Dan, *The Da Vinci Code*, Bantam, New York, 2003. This is the book that focused massive attention on the significance of Mary Magdalene. A well-written and absorbing thriller.

Browne, Sylvia, *The Two Marys: The hidden history of the Wife and Mother of Jesus*, Piatkus, London, 2008. A unique perspective on the lives of two of the most important women in the life of Jesus.

Cannon, Dolores, *Jesus and the Essenes*, Ozark Mountain Publishing, Huntsville, AR, 2000 (original UK edition 1992). The first big breakthrough on regression material from Essene lives. Gives a detailed account of Qumran and much insight into the reality of Essene life. Highly recommended.

Carroll, Lee and Tober, Jan, *The Indigo Children: The New Kids Have Arrived*, Hay House, Carlsbad, CA, 1999. The classic introduction to the subject of Indigo Children.

Cooper, Diana, *A New Light on Ascension*, Findhorn Press, Forres, Scotland, 2004. Written in a clear and direct style, this is much the best introduction to the whole field of ascension. Highly recommended.

Gardner, Laurence, *The Magdalene Legacy*, Element, London, 2005. A beautifully written and thoroughly researched survey of all the main sources in Magdalene scholarship.

Heartsong, Claire, *Anna, Grandmother of Jesus: A Message of Wisdom and Love*, S.E.E. Publishing, Santa Clara, CA, 2002. A wise and profound book casting light on a vital part of the family heritage of Jesus.

Hilarion, *The Letters of Paul: A New Interpretation for Modern Times*, 0 Books, Winchester and New York, 2005. Letters channeled by Sylvia Moss which give a new perspective on Paul's life and work. Informative, lucid and full of insight.

Holbeche, Soozi, *Changes: A Guide to Personal Transformation and New Ways of Living in the Next Millennium*, Piatkus, London, 1997. A book full of insight and practical tools to help us understand and manage the process of change.

Hurtak, James J, and Bozzoli, Jean-Luc, *Merkabah: Voyage of a Star Seed* (DVD), Academy for Future Science, Los Gatos, CA, 1998. A powerful visual presentation of the essential ideas in Hurtak's classic text *The Keys of Enoch*. Shows how sacred geometric designs move, develop and flow. Highly recommended as a means of expanding consciousness.

Ingram, Julia, *The Lost Sisterhood: The Return of Mary Magdalene, the Mother Mary and Other Holy Women*, Dreamspeaker Creations, Fort Collins, CO, 2004. This book, based on a whole series of past life regressions, puts the female perspective back into the accounts of the Ministry of Jeshua.

Kinster, Clysta, *Mary Magdalene, Beloved Disciple*, Cygnus Books, Llandeilo, 2005. A novel which sets Yeshua within the framework of the Osiris myth. A remarkable book, beautifully and sensitively written.

Losey, Meg Blackburn, *The Children of Now: Crystalline Children, Indigo Children, Star Kids, Angels on Earth, and the Phenomenon of Transitional Children*, New Page Books, Franklin Lakes, NJ, 2007. A thorough, practical and insightful survey of the New Children. Particularly good on the Crystal Children and on "Transitionals".

Matthews, Pamela, and Symons, Richard, *Goddesses of the New Light: A Goddess-a-Day Cards*, www.grail.co.nz, 2000. A magnificent 28-card oracle system celebrating Goddess energies with paintings by leading visionary artist Pamela Matthews. Highly recommended.

McGowan, Kathleen, *The Expected One*, Simon & Schuster, London, 2006. An intriguing novel based on research into the Magdalene lineage, and set mainly in the Cathar region of southern France.

Melchizedek, Drunvalo, *The Ancient Secret of the Flower of Life*, (2 volumes), Light Technology Publishing, Flagstaff, AZ, 1998 and 2000. The best modern text on relating sacred geometry to the process of spiritual transformation.

Melchizedek, Drunvalo, *Living in the Heart: How to Enter into the Sacred Space within the Heart*, Light Technology Publishing, Flagstaff, AZ, 2003. A book and audio CD combination which provides a meditational process for transformation.

Melchizedek, Drunvalo, *Serpent of Light: The Movement of the Earth's Kundalini and the Rise of the Female Light, 1949 to 2013*, Weiser Books, San Francisco, CA, 2007. A remarkable book to help us on our path and ease the process of transition.

Picknett, Lynn, *Mary Magdalene: Christianity's Hidden Goddess*, Robinson, London, 2003. A controversial and fascinating book which describes Mary as a leading disciple and the wife of Jesus.

Starbird, Margaret, *The Goddess in the Gospels: Reclaiming the Sacred Feminine*, Bear and Co., Rochester, VT, 1998. A profound and courageous book which re-examines the role of the sacred feminine in the early years of Christianity.

Virtue, Doreen, *The Crystal Children: A Guide to the Newest Generation of Psychic and Sensitive Children*, Hay House, Carlsbad, CA, 2003. An excellent introduction to the whole area of Crystal Children.

Virtue, Doreen, *Indigo, Crystal and Rainbow Children: A Guide to the New Generations of Highly Sensitive Young People*, (set of two audio CDs), Hay House, Carlsbad, CA, 2005. An informative live lecture by the world's leading authority on the new children.

Whitworth, Belinda, *New Age Encyclopedia: A Mind-Body-Spirit Reference Guide*, New Page Books, Franklin Lakes, NJ, 2003 and Robert Hale, London, 2005. An essential source-book for any seeker in this time of transformation.

Wilson, Stuart and Prentis, Joanna, *The Essenes, Children of the Light*, Ozark Mountain Publishing, Huntsville, AR, 2005. This was our first book, giving information on Essene links with the Druids, the existence of a secret Core Group around Jesus, and the real part played by Joseph of Arimathea.

Note 1: Some of the books cited above (especially the more esoteric titles) may be difficult to source from general bookshops.

They can be obtained from Arcturus Books at www.arcturusbooks.co.uk, phone 01803 864363, from Aristia at www.aristia.co.uk, phone 01983 721060, or from Cygnus at www.cygnus-books.co.uk, phone 01550 777701.

Note 2: Further information on the New Children can be accessed through the websites listed on our website (see Feedback From Readers section.) Many useful websites can also be found in the Appendix to *The Children of Now* by Meg Blackburn Losey.

Acknowledgments

We would like to say a big "thank you" to all those whose past life experiences form the core of this book: your input was essential and there would have been no book without you:

Cathie Welchman
Isabel Zaplana
Michael Schaefer
Ingrid Brechtel
Emma
Bina
Margaret

A special "thank you" to Jennifer Crews for contributing the chapter on *Understanding the New Children*. So much of what Jennifer says confirms our own research, and her extensive experience of working with the new children makes her highly qualified to write this insightful assessment. It is remarkable how much her practical experience as a professional in this field backs up what Alariel says about the new children.

A big "thank you" to Isabel Zaplana and Michael Schaefer for all their help and support. Isabel proved to be a most brilliant and tireless translator, making our German session a real success.

Our special thanks to Cathie Welchman for her friendship and support, particularly in our investigation of Light Conception, where her training as a biologist was an essential component in the research process. Cathie can be contacted through her website, www.gaiaessences.com.

Our thanks to the many friends who have been supportive of our work, particularly Lyn and Graham Whiteman, Pamela Matthews and Richard Symons, Jackie Dixon, Anne MacEwen, Sylvia Moss and Chrissie Astell.

Joanna writes: I am grateful to Antony Delahay for gracefully accepting the amount of time I have spent on researching and producing this book. Thank you, Antony!

Many thanks to those whose feedback from our first book enabled us to extend our research, especially Gaynel Andrusko, Jim in Brisbane, William Brune in Missouri and Bernadette in Australia. And our thanks to the many readers who are continuing to contact us.

Feedback from Readers

Please let us know what you feel about this book as that feedback may help us when developing future books. You can contact us through our website:

www.foundationforcrystalchildren.com

We are open to receiving questions from readers: just email them to us and we will put them to Alariel at an appropriate time. Please bear in mind that Alariel does not take personal questions, or make predictions about the future of individuals or groups. If the answers are interesting, we may wish (with your approval) to feature them in some future book.

Index

patronymic names 19
Paz, Uzi 82
Peter the disciple 89, 99
Pharisees 8, 86, 114
Philip the disciple 84, 89, 99, 151
Pierre, a monk in France 133
prayer 26
Preseli 52
princess 59

Qumran 10

Rainbow Children 183
Rebekah, sister of Mary Anna 84, 151
resurrection 119
Ruth: see Laura Clare

Sacred Feminine 27
Sara, daughter of Isaac 84, 151
Sarah-Anna 144, 150
Schaefer, Michael, a past life subject 53
Schori, Katharine 91
soul aspects 27
soul family 93
Starlight Centre, the 3
Steiner Education 189
Stonehenge 52
Sufi movement 100
Super-Psychic Children 182
Susannah Mary 85

Tabitha, wife of Isaac 143
Tai Chi 15

Tamar Miriam, a cousin of Jeshua 146
Technology of Light 239
Thomas the disciple 89, 99, 116
time 25
tin 18, 80
Tomb, healing in the 78

Unconditional Love 86, 105, 109, 239

Wales 52
Way, the 88, 99, 114
Web of life 230
Welchman, Cathie 4, 31, 109, 117, 151
Wild Flowers of the Holy Land 82

Yogananda 116
yogi 118

Zaplana, Isabel, a past life subject 11, 53, 167
Zealots 87
Zohar, the 51

About the Authors

Stuart Wilson is a writer on new perspectives and the author of the best-selling name dictionary *Simply the Best Baby Name Book*. His perceptions of the new consciousness have been developed through 30 years of working with groups committed to personal growth. For nine years, Stuart co-focalized (with Joanna Prentis) the Starlight Centre in the West of England, a centre dedicated to healing and the trans-formation of consciousness.

He writes about this period:

> It was inspiring and fascinating but also exhaust ing! A stream of visitors came in to the Centre, mainly from the United States and Australia, but some also from Europe. We had an amazing and mind-bending time sitting at the feet of interna tionally respected spiritual teachers and workshop leaders.

Part of the work of the Centre was research into past lives, and this led to his collaboration with Joanna to write *The Essenes, Children of the Light* (published by Ozark Mountain Publishing in 2005.) Based on the past life regres-sion of 7 subjects, this book reveals Essene links with the Druids, the existence of a secret Core Group around Jesus, and contacts with the Order of Melchizedek.

You can visit Stuart at his website:
www.foundationforcrystalchildren.com

Joanna Prentis: I was born in Bangalore in southern India. When I was nearly three, my family returned to Scotland where I spent my childhood and teenage years. After leaving school, I traveled extensively, married and lived in Hong Kong for two years and then ten years in the bush in Western Australia, where my three daughters were born. It was there that my interest began in alternative medicine and education, organic farming, metaphysics and meditation. With a local nurse, we ran a Homeopathic and Radionic practice.

I returned to the UK in 1979 and later trained as a Montessori teacher, educating my two youngest daughters, Katinka and Larissa, at home for a few years. I now have three beautiful grandchildren.

I did several healing courses and have a foundation diploma in Humanistic Psychology. I also trained with Ursula Markham and have a diploma in Hypnotherapy and Past Life Therapy.

With my eldest daughter Tatanya, I set up the Starlight Centre in 1988, a centre for healing and the expansion of consciousness. Over the years, Tatanya has introduced us to many innovative techniques and interesting people.

In 1999, we closed the Centre to focus on producing our books. I continue with my Past Life work, and readers now connect with us from all over the world.

You can visit Joanna at her website:
www.foundationforcrystalchildren.com